# HE HEALETH

# THE

# WOUNDED HEART

## Emotional Healing
## Through the Atonement of
## Jesus Christ

He Healeth the Wounded Heart
© 2012
by D. Ryan Porter

First Printing © 2009
Entitled "Emotional Healing"

DRP Publishing
drppublishing.com
drporter21@gmail.com

He Healeth the Wounded Heart
ISBN-13: 978-0-9853140-0-2

Printed in the United States of America

Note: This book is not intended to replace the advice or care of professional health care practitioners.

# CONTENTS

# APPENDICES

# EMOTIONAL ABUSE

**A**ngela *dislikes* being alone. She clings to those that show interest and is always focused on how they can make her feel better. She bases her feelings of self-worth on others' opinion of her. She expects those close to her to know her needs and to spend time fulfilling them. She develops strategies to make others feel guilty for not meeting her needs. She is only happy when others meet her expectations.

*Tom fears* commitment. He has dated many women but finds that it is difficult to be open with his feelings and make the marriage commitment. Even when he is attracted to a woman, he is fearful and uneasy about the possibility of marriage. He is concerned that if he commits to marriage it might not work out.

*Madeline overdoes it* trying to be everything to everyone. She feels guilty when she cannot meet perceived expectations. She believes she must be perfect to be happy and is overwhelmed by the attempt. She watches other women serve the needy, be patient with their children and husbands, and maintain cleanliness and order in their homes. She never measures up to the other women around her. She sometimes takes pleasure in others' failures and feels guilty for doing so. When her children choose poorly or get into trouble, she blames herself for their failures. Even when she is doing all she can, she is never really happy or satisfied with her life.

*Jacob has been struggling* with a pornography addiction for many years. He tries to justify his addiction by saying that it is not fornication or adultery and it does not often occur. Justification does not help. He still feels dirty and unworthy each time he views and does all he can to hide his secret. He berates himself and does not understand why he cannot quit and give it up. He pleads again and again with God to help him stop. He has tried to increase his efforts to do everything else right in his life to make up for his problem. It seems like there are few if any answers, and he struggles with feelings of despair.

*April has difficulty* maintaining relationships. She has divorced twice and finds it hard to trust others. She is very uncomfortable in a crowd. She does not attempt to control her weight or to make herself attractive. She feels intense anger that comes from nowhere and for no reason. She believes that God is not helping, and she questions her faith in God.

*Lisa's anger was more* than she could cope with. One day, after she had been married for a little more than a year, she broke out all of the windows in the house and set fire to her living room chair. When the fire truck arrived she was waiting for the fire to overtake her.

**Bill works hard** to fulfill his church responsibilities. He has difficulty holding a job. He has never been able to sustain his interest in a profession. He sees himself as a constant failure. He views his life as black and white and believes that God will ultimately reject him. He projects his feelings onto others and cannot understand why they are not more like him. He finds that he constantly feels depressed and unworthy. Occasionally, he is nearly incapacitated by bouts of depression. He gets angry at the slightest provocation and wrestles with himself to keep control. He "white-knuckles it" to meet his commitments. He vacillates between minor addictions to movies, video games, sodas, and food. He feels an inner pain and heartache but does not understand it.

**Mandy struggles** to get out of bed each morning. She knows that keeping the commandments of God should bring happiness but she always feels sadness. She struggles to find joy in any activity. She wonders if the world would be a better place without her. She has lost hope for the future and feels pain in the present.

These are just a few cases that reflect some of the effects of emotional trauma or abuse. All forms of abuse are emotional. There is not a living soul that has not experienced some type of emotional trauma. There is no way to avoid it. Emotional trauma is an inherent part of life and provides growth. What we may not realize is that we develop patterns of behavior based on our perception of life's experiences. These underlying beliefs become our master, and much of life's experiences are an outgrowth and reflection of our core beliefs; beliefs often acquired in our youth. There are always emotions tied to our

3

experiences. When exposed to various types of traumatic experiences, we invariably develop some incorrect patterns of behavior and irrational thoughts. The intensity of emotion attached to a trauma is very much determined by the sensitivity of the individual and the magnitude of the abuse.

The following are a few examples of traumas that could bring about the patterns of behavior and thoughts exemplified in some of the examples above.

1) Physically hurt in an accident or seeing someone else hurt.

2) Exposed to information not age-appropriate. An example might be when a child is exposed to pornography or is told information that he or she is not mature enough to process.

3) Called degrading names, belittled, always disapproved of, and blamed.

4) Experienced the loss of a loved one or close friend in death or divorce.

5) Experienced the divorce of one's parents.

6) Unable to gain parental or spousal approval.

7) Required to fill the role of an adult in the family although still a child.

8) Sexually molested.

9) Physically beaten, hurt, or tortured.

10) Imprisoned, starved or humiliated as punishment or to inflict hurt.

11) Observing parents and siblings hurt themselves and other family members through addictions, arguing, fighting, and other destructive behaviors.

12) Life changing events such as moving to a new home, a new baby, a new school, or a new stepparent.

13) Lack of affection or validation during childhood or as an adult.

The different ways we can experience emotional trauma are innumerable. Sometimes the trauma may be something as simple as unexpected or undesirable change. Suffice it to say, we have all experienced emotional trauma, intentional and unintentional, at some time in our lives.

The individuals in these examples could be any of us. We all have our own story about our struggle to follow the Savior and our need to heal our hearts. Throughout this book I attempt to teach that, whenever we obtain healing, Jesus Christ is the healer. He is exactly who he and the prophets say he is, and he has the power to heal our lives. However, many people struggle to find answers to their problems and cannot make changes in their lives. Some blame religion and determine the gospel of Christ could not be true because they continue to come up spiritually and emotionally empty, even after wrestling with the Lord in prayer and trying to keep the commandments. Some even blame God for not caring enough to help them. They do not understand why the gospel does not seem to bring the peace they seek.

I spent years struggling with many of these same questions. It seemed my prayers were empty and the darkness would never lift. I could not understand why the Lord would not hear and answer me. I later discovered that he had heard every one of my prayers and designed a way for me to progress. I also discovered that the Lord blesses us for our persistence and patience, even when we feel like our prayers seem to be ineffective. "**In your patience possess ye your souls**" (Luke 21:19). This book is based on a few of the things I have learned during my personal journey. Your journey will be different from mine, but the Savior will always be the common denominator, the source of all true healing.

My thoughts and ideas were not developed in a classroom, although I have read many things relating to the topic of emotional healing. My qualifications are my own experiences, the experiences of others, and much observation. My personal experience takes me through abuse as a young child, severe depression as an adult, operating a treatment center with emotionally challenged juvenile offenders, coursework in psychology, counseling adults and youth inside and outside of the church, observing professional and non-professional counselors, possessing a thirst for personal healing, and experiencing first hand the life changing emotional healing power of the Atonement of Jesus Christ.

My intent is to inspire within each of us the reflection and introspection necessary to **"know even as also [we are] known"** (1 Corinthians 13:12). In other words, to see ourselves as God sees us and discover the healing we need to progress and partake of the Savior's grace. There are many books that attempt to answer questions people have about why they continue to feel and behave the way they do. I want to demonstrate that emotional, spiritual, and sometimes even physical healing principles are based in the ancient and modern day scriptures. It still seems strange to me that I had to discover many of these principles outside of a religious setting and the scriptures to realize that they were right in front of me all along in the Gospel of Jesus Christ. My hope is that we will realize that the Gospel is the basis for any real change we make. Healing principles may be presented in different ways, but when we break them down, it always comes back to the teachings of the Savior and his Atonement.

Some of the effective healing therapies we hear about are often contained in the scriptures. For example, visualization, a very powerful modality, is taught in Alma chapter 5. Alma encourages us to visualize with words such as **"can ye imagine"** and **"can ye think"** and **"can ye look" (Alma 5:18-20).** Many people do not see these ideas in the scriptures for what they may represent in relation to healing.

You may still be thinking to yourself that you have never been through any type of emotional trauma, and this book may not apply to you. However, everyone deals with painful emotions and incorrect thinking and negative patterns of behavior in some form or another. For example, you may have been cheated in business, you may have had an unfaithful spouse, your child may be involved in drugs, or you may have lost a loved one in a drunk driving accident. We all need to forgive ourselves and others, and the Savior wants us all to experience his Atonement and love. Healing our hearts takes place when we apply the principles of the Atonement. The Atonement is the very essence of the Gospel of Jesus Christ. The Prophet Joseph Smith said, "The Atonement is the most important single thing that has ever occurred in the entire history of created things; it is the rock [solid] foundation upon which the gospel and all other things rest. Indeed, all things which pertain to our religion are only appendages to it." [1] If this is so we should spend our lives trying to understand and partake of the Atonement of Jesus Christ.

In these few pages, I want to share some of the ways I personally have applied the principles of the Atonement in my life. I will comment on the effects of emotional pain and healing and identify principles and ideas set forth in the scriptures that may help unlock the Atonement in your life. The following chapters will provide principles for change as well as specific strategies to apply these principles. I want to open your mind to these concepts and possibilities and encourage you to turn to the Savior for healing. All of the principles and discussion set forth in this work have but one purpose: to heal and change the heart.

Even though many techniques used by mainstream and alternative practitioners benefit our healing, there are also many techniques that offend our souls and do us harm. Several years ago while working with juvenile delinquents, I toured the sex offender program for adults and youth at a well-known hospital in Phoenix, Arizona. I was disturbed by the methods used to treat these individuals. One method employed, which is still a standard practice today, was to expose sex offenders to highly offensive pornographic images in an effort to measure sexual arousal. Satan could not have designed a more deviant testing procedure. The professionals also required sex offenders to attend group meetings and discuss their sexual fantasies. They would group even the mildest sex offenders with the most deviant offenders during these sessions. The thought comes to my mind that with both of these methods of treatment they are trying to treat the sickness by not only exposing offenders to the disease, but also by exposing them to an advanced disease these offenders may have never experienced or thought of before.

It is important to ask God to direct our path as we consider healing alternatives. We are shown **"the way to judge; for every thing which inviteth to do good, and to persuade to believe in Christ, is sent forth by the power and gift of Christ; wherefore ye may know with a perfect knowledge it is of God" (Moroni 7:16).** The Lord is telling us that whatever alternatives we study or apply should be something that will lead us to Christ.

There are numerous books that provide detail on different methods of healing and discuss other concepts of healing that may be helpful. I do not attempt to convey all the concepts that may help you along the healing path. Truth can be found in many places but not all that you read will be truth. For example, many healers teach reincarnation. I do not believe in reincarnation and consider it to be contrary to the teachings and plan of God.

We must study and pray about what we read, and have the spirit confirm the true principles to our hearts and minds. We are all entitled to receive personal revelation from God. **"Ask, and it shall be given you; seek, and ye shall find; knock, and it shall be opened. For everyone that asketh receiveth; and he that seeketh findeth;**

9

**and to him that knocketh it shall be opened" (Matt 7:7-8). "If any of you lack wisdom, let him ask of God, that giveth to all men liberally, and upbraideth not; and it shall be given him" (James 1:5).** God is willing to teach us the truth if we are willing to seek it out. I do not present my ideas as confirmed truth or doctrine, and I state many personal opinions, although I do believe in the concepts presented here. I encourage you to pray about what you read in this book that you may gain wisdom from God.

I begin this short work by bearing my witness that the Atonement is real, and that it is necessary for salvation. Every soul must partake of it to be healed and redeemed. Jesus Christ is not a myth or just a great prophet, but the Lord and Savior of all mankind. His love for you and I was perfected through the great suffering he endured on our behalf that enabled mercy to satisfy justice. Our love for him will also be perfected over time as we experience the Atonement and learn to endure our own suffering with patience and gratitude. We each **"[endure] the crosses of the world"** through our seeking, our getting back up after failure, the everyday struggles, the pain of trials, the striving for answers, the not knowing, and the willingness to continue repenting and forgiving, even when it seems impossible. These things produce within us the **"kingdom of God"** and allow us to be like him **(2 Nephi 9:18).** The most effective emotional work is done with the guidance of the Spirit of the Lord. The Savior is the only one that can **"take away the guilt from our hearts"** and relieve our pain **(Alma 24:10).** Know that we may not always be healed from certain ailments while in the flesh, but God promises he will heal our hearts if we ask. **"A new heart also will I give you and a new spirit will I put within you"** **(Ezekiel 36:26).** By acquiring a new heart we become better servants of God and our fellow man.

Understand that this book may only provide some of the answers you are seeking. Do not despair. Continue to plead and call upon God. He hears every prayer and knows your need. As you begin to seek healing, you should realize that God's ways are not your ways. Things may even appear to be moving away from your desired outcome and getting worse. Try to keep faith that the Lord knows what he is doing and thank him for any change, even if it is against all that you hoped for or expected. Be assured that he will design a path for change that will bring you the greatest blessings.

# TRUTH

Truth is the very foundation of emotional healing. As Jesus spoke to a group of Jews who believed on him, he stated that if they continued in his word they would **"know the truth, and the truth shall make you free" (John 8:32).** This freedom is all-inclusive. Knowing the truth provides freedom from the bondage of false perceptions, feelings of abandonment, emotional suffering, darkness of mind, depression, hate, anger, sin, addiction, mental, physical and spiritual limitations, disbelief, pride, negative attitudes, low self-worth, sickness, etc... The list is infinite.

Truth is sometimes difficult to recognize and identify because our actions and thoughts may be founded on misperceptions, a lack of truth, or a distortion of truth. One way this might occur is because of our perception of specific events. For example, when I was six, my parents failed to return home before dark one rainy evening. I believed that they had been killed and would never return. I remember sobbing for two hours as I gazed out the window into the rainy darkness. I was later able to see some connection to future irrational thoughts and my fearful attitudes under certain circumstances.

A distortion of truth might also occur when we sin or we are misguided by others. **"And that wicked one cometh and taketh away light and truth, through disobedience, from the children of men, and because of the traditions of their fathers" (D&C 93:39).** "Fathers" may include anyone who is in a role of authority over another or has influence over another. Satan takes away the truth and light in our lives when we are abused, mistreated, or when we disregard truth and conscience through sin and disobedience. Parents may also unknowingly divert light and truth from their children when they struggle with emotional issues themselves.

For example, a father may honestly believe that because he is the head of the family he should make all of the decisions. He expects the family members to follow and obey him without a say or a voice. He might actually believe that the Lord wants him to take charge in this way, and he enforces his decisions through various types of physical, spiritual, or emotional punishment.

Let us carry this further to see how this takes away light and truth. The man's wife may become extremely angry with the children and lash out verbally and physically because of the frustration and hurt she feels under the harsh rule of her controlling husband. She feels deceived, having believed that a temple marriage would bring happiness and love into her home. She feels no joy in the Gospel or in her family.

The children may become depressed or act out inappropriately; seeking ways to alleviate the emotional pain they feel through involvement in sex, drugs or even self-mutilation. Their image of God becomes distorted and their joy in the gospel is crushed. The truth becomes dimmer and dimmer in their lives. They often turn from God and the gospel considering them to be the reason for their pain. Realizing that many families are dysfunctional, and that light and truth are being extinguished, we need to strive to follow the Savior's admonition to "teach ye diligently" while serving as leaders and teachers in the church. We may provide truth and light that may not be available in the home.

We will continue to discuss in later chapters why and how both committing sin and being an innocent victim of others' acts removes light and truth in our lives. These positions are such opposites, yet both require the healing power of the Atonement.

Here are a few questions we might ask ourselves to see if light and truth have been distorted or taken from our lives.

Do I feel sadness and depression as a general rule?

Am I stuck in negative or addictive patterns of behavior?

Am I often battling anger? Do I have a short fuse?

Do I constantly degrade myself with negative self-talk?

Do I self-medicate with drugs, pornography, media, food, self-mutilation or other addictions to relieve loneliness, guilt, pain, hurt, anger or other negative emotions?

Am I stuck on a plateau and cannot seem to progress?

Do I lack motivation to change?

Is failure the pattern of my life's experiences?

Do I find it hard to express my negative emotions and understand my negative actions?
Do I hurt others emotionally and wonder why I do so?
Am I unable to stand up for myself?
Do I overachieve to compensate for feelings of poor self-image?

Truth is power, and truth will always be revealed to those who seek it and are ready and willing to apply it. For one to see as God sees, **"Let him that is ignorant learn wisdom by humbling himself and calling upon the Lord his God, that his eyes may be opened that he may see, and his ears opened that he may hear" (D&C 136:32).** "But unto him that keepeth my commandments I will give the mysteries of my kingdom, and the same shall be in him a well of living water, springing up unto everlasting life" (D&C 63:23). Wisdom and the mysteries of the kingdom are synonymous with light and truth. These scriptures outline a few helps to obtain truth. They tell us to be humble, call upon the Lord, and keep the commandments. These steps are important but what if we struggle to do them right now, or what if we do and nothing seems to change? What if we keep trying to live the commandments but continue to make the same mistakes? What if we pray for hours but the pain or the guilt just will not dissipate? What if we keep trying but we struggle unsuccessfully to change our feelings toward another or to feel God's love?

This does not mean that the scriptures are false or that the promises of the Lord are not true. It might be that we do not understand humility or even know how to pray or what to pray for. It might be that our concept of God is so irrational and our belief in the way that he should help us so distorted that faith in his mercy is nearly impossible. It might be that light and truth are so dim within us that we do not know how to retrieve it. Sometimes we might need help from a leader, a friend, a professional or possibly a book to begin the healing process and get our bearings.

Even under these circumstances, let me assure you that God does hear and provide answers, and he can help us on whatever level we are at and with whatever shortcomings we may have. There are also reasons he answers the way he does. He answers in the way that we can best learn and grow.

I recall pouring my soul out to God in the depths of depression and feeling abandoned and forgotten. Day after day I sought relief and found very little. Little did I know that somewhere, somehow, God was preparing the way for me to learn, make changes, and begin healing. I believe that my prayers, even while I was angry with God, were heard, and they set in motion the events and learning that would change my life. **"And thus I will do unto thee because this long time ye have cried unto me" (Ether 1:43).** It is hard to be patient and continue to call upon God when we are in pain, but we must persist in seeking his help.

There are two types of truth that will allow us to heal and become whole. The first type of truth is general or universal truth, ideas and concepts that apply to everyone, all mankind. No one is excluded from the requirement to know these truths. They must be applied in every person's life for that person to obtain salvation or healing. They are understood through personal revelation.

Salvation and healing are interchangeable because true emotional and spiritual healing is really a process of forgiveness and repentance, without which no man or woman can be saved. Emotional healing is a spiritual process, **"All things unto [God] are spiritual" (D&C 29:34).** One example of universal truth is the Atonement of Jesus Christ. It is extended to everyone and all mankind will be affected by it.

Another example of universal truth is the nature of God. One of the irrational thoughts I struggled with most was that God was a severe God. In my mind, he was a God that expected me to be perfect or he would cast me off forever. My life was completely filled with guilt and fear. God teaches us, **"Their fear towards me is taught by the precepts of men" (2 Nephi 27:25).** I never felt worthy no matter what I did. I finally decided that I did not want to worship or even be with such a being in the next life. However, I still prayed and struggled to understand God's nature.

One evening in the dreams of the night, I experienced the pure love of God for myself and realized that his love extended to even the vilest sinner and the most mistreated individuals. The feeling was so intense and all encompassing that I realized God was completely different from what I had believed. He wanted me to be with him, and I was here to grow and learn so I could be like him. I was not on earth to arrive at the end of my life only to be cast off and forever burning in a bottomless pit. I realized I was here on earth to learn to love as he loves through my life's experiences and his example. This understanding of God's love is another universal truth that all people are entitled to know.

The second type of truth is personal or individual truth. This type of truth applies only to a specific person or persons. If it is difficult to think that some truths only apply to one individual or group and not another, consider the story of the people of Anti-Nephi-Lehi in Alma 53:10-21 of the Book of Mormon. These people made a covenant with God to show God that they had sincerely repented of the many murders they had committed prior to their conversion. They promised to never lift up their weapons of war against another people. Until their deaths this covenant was strictly obeyed, even at the peril and loss of their lives. Their children did not make the same covenant and were justified in taking up arms against their enemies in defense of their lives and liberty. We see that this truth only applied to the parents, not the children.

In addition to creating personal truths through personal covenants that we choose to make with God, the Holy Ghost reveals, by other methods, personal truths to individuals regarding their specific situations and life circumstances. These truths often allow us to change our perceptions about God, others, events, and ourselves. With changes in perception come transformations in our emotions. This is an important key to healing. For example, the Lord may reveal to us specific reasons a particular event took place in our lives or he may reveal an unknown truth about a specific person who has offended us. This new information may allow us to perceive a person differently or look at the event in a totally different context.

Revealed personal truth may also help us realize the blessings and strengths that we have received and developed because of certain mistreatments and trials. Often those who have suffered the most demonstrate the greatest compassion. Consider the Savior. **"He will take upon him the pains and the sicknesses of his people. ...And he will take upon him their infirmities, that his bowels may be filled with mercy" (Alma 9:11-12)** Because of his tremendous suffering he can love and feel compassion on a level little understood by humanity.

The Savior understood our need to fill our hearts with compassion when he revealed to Joseph Smith that the Disciples of Christ **"forgave not one another in their hearts" (D&C 64:8)**. Herein lies an important key or formula for emotional healing. To change the heart we must have a change in our emotions or feelings so that we truly feel compassion. To change our feelings we must experience a change in our perception. To change our perception we must see and understand the truth, and all truth is a gift from God. God will reveal the truth that will heal our heart and allow us to forgive in our heart. We must be able to see ourselves and others as Christ does.

The following examples illustrate how truth can be revealed and change our perceptions and therefore our feelings.

I was talking with a woman who had been sexually abused. She related that some years after the abuse occurred she had a very lucid dream wherein she saw her perpetrator being severely abused by others, even more so than the abuse inflicted upon her. She said that at the time of this dream she could finally feel compassion for the abuser, and she felt the release of negative emotions associated with the abuse.

Several years ago I became aware of a woman who was abused by her father at an early age. She had not seen him in over 15 years. The first time I spoke to her about him she would say very little and was extremely angry. As I gently encouraged her she began a slow process of forgiveness. I told her that her father had made many changes in his life, and asked her to meet with the two of us for a few minutes to allow him to apologize. After several months of coaxing she finally agreed. At the conclusion of this meeting, she confided in me that he was a totally different man from the father she had known. She could see and feel his humility and sorrow for his misdeeds. Her perception and feelings about him had changed and her heart was softened. A few months later, I received a call from a very excited father telling me that he had been invited over to his daughter's home for the holiday, and that they both had enjoyed their time together very much. She had discovered a truth about her father that had changed her perception, creating compassion, and allowing true forgiveness in her heart.

I realize that not all those who offend will ask forgiveness or repent. Many may continue in their offensive behavior and may not, according to our opinion, deserve compassion. If this is the case, it is important that we seek the truth about the way Jesus Christ views these individuals. Remember, Christ loves all God's children, even the offender.

Let me share one final example relating to perception. One evening I went to the temple with my son-in-law. As we were coming into the locker room, he discovered that someone was in his locker. He waited and waited and waited. I had time to go to my locker and change and come back out while he was waiting. Finally, the man exited the locker. We could see that he was handicapped and unable to perform basic functions, such as changing clothes in a routine way. My son-in-law later related to me that he had been getting a little upset that it had taken this person so long to change. The longer he waited the more it bothered him. When the man emerged, the realization of the situation (truth) became apparent and his perception and therefore his feelings completely changed. He was embarrassed and felt very humbled that he had experienced these feelings. He did not have to force himself to feel compassion or patience. It was a natural result of understanding the truth.

It is only through the knowledge and right application of truth that we can heal our lives and change our behavior. The Lord intends our healing to be a personal discovery process. It must be so that we can grow. God will provide answers for us, but he first requires that we take action. **"Ask, and it shall be given you; seek, and ye shall find; knock, and it shall be opened unto you" (Matt 7:7).** We must ask and knock for him to open the door. The Lord of the house needs to know that we are without the door attempting to come in; otherwise there is no reason for him to open the door.

I have noticed that every time the Lord reveals something in my own life, it is because I specifically asked a question. Every dream or revelation I have received was a direct result of asking God a specific question. The

Prophet Joseph Smith is a perfect example of this. He received the vision of God the Father and Jesus Christ because he asked a question. He received the visit of John the Baptist because he asked about baptism. All the revelations Joseph Smith received in the Doctrine and Covenants were received as a result of asking specific questions. We must do the same to discover truth.

Healing truths will be revealed in different ways to different people. They may come through dreams, visions, inspiration, others placed in our path, the study of good books, observation, or the application of correct principles. As Brigham Young stated, "Our doctrine and practice is, and I have made it mine through life...to receive truth no matter where it comes from." [2] We must seek with real intent to find our answers no mater where the source.

Let us not limit our search for truth as the Jews did during the time of Christ. They could not see beyond the Law of Moses when Christ offered a greater law, even though the Law of Moses was symbolic of the Savior's great sacrifice. They could not take their focus off traditions, customs and what seemed to be the normal way of doing things. They completely missed the most important event of all time, the Atonement of Jesus Christ.

# WHY HEAL EMOTIONALLY?

There are many reasons we need to heal our negative emotions. One very important reason is so that we can make lasting changes in our lives. We all know what it feels like to fail again and again battling the same issues. As long as we hold on to emotional pain, we are locked in negative patterns and progress slowly. Holding in or suppressing negative feelings blocks truth and light and leads to darkness and the inability to fully feel the spirit. How does this happen? Negative emotions consist of negative energy or negative matter, and when we hold on to these emotions they become locked in different areas of the body. They are uncomfortable and can cause disease and physical problems such as migraines, ulcers, heart conditions, and many other health issues. They also diffuse and partially block the light of Christ and the influence of the Holy Ghost. When our emotions are intensely negative they block the spirit and

23

we operate from a position of need and want instead of acting from a position of love, giving, and strength.

When we are needy our thoughts become warped and irrational. We look at everything with an attitude of how can I get love, how do I appear to others, how can I gain acceptance, how can I be recognized for what I have done and how can I impress others so that I feel as if I have value and worth? These thoughts cause us to act out inappropriately in an attempt to receive attention, fill the loneliness, and minimize the pain and hurt. Satan quickly tells us lies to drive us further into the dark. He wants to block the truth, and he has the opportunity to do so as we feel more worthless and unlovable.

Many of us have never been allowed to express negative feelings in a beneficial way or had our feelings validated by being recognized as something we are permitted to feel. For example, if a young boy tells his father he is scared, the father will say, "Big boys aren't scared," or "There is nothing to be scared of." He discounts his son's emotions by saying it is not okay to feel fear. The boy soon chooses not to express his feelings, and when he does have feelings he sees them as a bad thing. He begins a process of holding in negative emotions that block the light of Christ.

As a result of holding in feelings, many of us develop negative patterns of reacting to painful experiences. For example, a woman has trouble trusting future suitors after a painful divorce or a child fears abandonment in relationships after losing a parent. David Viscot provides the following helpful definitions. Anxiety is "future hurt or the expectation of hurt or loss." Hurt is "present pain or the experience of loss or injury." Shame/Guilt is "past pain unexpressed or anger held in and turned against yourself." Depression is "past pain — chronically unexpressed."[3] As unexpressed and unresolved feelings linger and intensify, they lead to many unwanted thoughts and behaviors. Below are just a few of these feelings and behaviors.

| | | |
|---|---|---|
| Abusive | Addicted | Angry |
| Appearance Issues | Avoidance | Blaming |
| Confused | Controlling | Dependent |
| Depressed | Destructive | Explosive |
| Failure Patterns | Poor Self-Image | Guilty |
| Irrational Thoughts | Resentment | Mistrusting |
| Perfectionism | Unworthy | Fearful |
| Unlovable | Judgmental | Victimized |

Unresolved negative emotions generally keep us from living the Gospel of Jesus Christ and loving God and others. Even when we try to live the gospel, we are not happy and cannot find peace. Sometimes we feel like the Gospel is the problem because it should bring us happiness. Some people leave the church because they are unable to attain the blessings and peace promised. We need to heal so that we can understand God and have peace and happiness in our lives. If we do not address the pain, our self-worth continues to deteriorate. In this condition, we continue to repeat negative patterns and cannot advance.

A second reason we need to seek emotional healing is to allow and accept the Atonement of Jesus

Christ into our lives. **"Thou art angry, O Lord, with this people, because they will not understand thy mercies which thou hast bestowed upon them because of thy Son" (Alma 33:16).** If we do not find a way to effectuate the Atonement, we are in reality, rejecting his gift and the suffering he has endured for our pain. **"He will take upon him the pains and the sicknesses of his people. ...And he will take upon him their infirmities... The Son of God suffereth according to the flesh that he might take upon him the sins of his people, that he might blot out their transgressions according to the power of his deliverance" (Alma 7:11-13).** The Savior's gift is one of infinite mercy and love designed to deliver us from our pain.

We accept the Atonement when we allow Christ to take the hurt, guilt, anger, loneliness, and pain we have carried around for so long. **"O Lord my God, I cried unto thee, and thou hast healed me" (Psalms 30:2).** Christ defined his role in our lives when he read from the scriptures in the synagogue. **"He hath sent me to heal the broken hearted, to preach deliverance to the captives, and recovering of sight to the blind, to set at liberty them that are bruised" (Luke 4:18).** Are we not all brokenhearted, captive, blind, and bruised in some way or another?

If we choose not to let the Savior have our pain and free us because we **"[exercise] no faith unto repentance,"** the demands of justice will exact their toll upon us every moment of every day. We are **"exposed to the whole law of the demands of justice."** Justice is not something that we will only experience in the next life; it is occurring this very moment. **"Therefore only unto him that has faith unto repentance is brought about the great and eternal plan of redemption" (Alma 34:16).** The Lord requires us to exercise faith to gain his forgiveness.

An abuse victim might believe they have nothing to repent of, but as long as we continue to feel shame, guilt, and anger we have not yet allowed the Atonement of Christ to heal our souls. We have not exercised faith unto repentance. This seems hard, especially to victims of someone else's sin and mistreatment, but the Atonement is designed for all men. **"I, the Lord, will forgive whom I will forgive, but of you it is required to forgive all men" (D&C 64:10).** God requires all to repent and forgive.

If a victim feels justified in holding resentment and hate, they are rejecting the Atonement. It may often seem impossible to turn this over to Christ, especially if we are currently living in abusive circumstances. Forgiveness is necessary for our own good, not only to free the offender but also to free ourselves and have peace and joy in this life and the next. If you are currently in an abusive relationship, forgiveness does not require that you allow the abuse to continue. It should be addressed and resolved as soon as possible. The Lord does not tolerate abuse of any kind.

I do not believe the Lord condones divorce or separation until all other options are exhausted, unless there is severe abuse or physical danger. If partners are willing and making efforts, consideration should be given to reconciliation. However, I know of women in the church who refused separation or divorce under extremely abusive conditions. They believed that they deserved their situation, would not be able to support or take care of their family, were going against the commandments, or felt sorry for the abusive husband. If you find yourself in such a situation, you need to consider all of the facts and the negative effects on your family members and upon yourself, and try to get direction from the Lord and a competent leader.

The third reason we must heal is that we will carry forward into the next life the same attitudes of bitterness, guilt, and shame that we harbor in this life. We may think that death will relieve us of these feelings, but it will not. The Lord tells us, **"That same spirit which doth possess your bodies at the time that ye go out of this life, that same spirit will have power to possess your body in that eternal world" (Alma 34:34).** Death is but a continuation of our earthly existence and progress.

Based on these teachings, suicide does not bring relief. If you choose suicide as a way out of your emotional pain, you will carry the pain and despair with you into the next life. You will increase your pain by having hurt loved ones and friends that you left behind. You will also deprive yourself of the growth opportunities you were to experience in mortality. Suicide is not a way out but a ploy used by Satan to destroy God's children.

Fourth, it is almost impossible to exercise true faith when we are locking in negative emotions. We "white-knuckle it" trying to follow a God that we may even resent for not taking better care of us. Since faith grows and manifests in our heart, negative emotions hinder faith. **"With the heart man believeth unto righteousness"**

28

**(Romans 10:10).** If our heart is not well we will struggle to believe.

Because of our experiences we may question why God would allow such things to happen. We cannot understand why he did not protect us or why he allowed us to be abandoned by the people who should have loved us. If we felt that God was not there in the past, why would he be there for us in the future? How can we ever trust in him again?

God is not the author of the ills we experience, and he will not prevent bad things from happening to innocent people. If he did so it would defeat the purpose of mortality. Some of the ills we experience are things that happen to people by virtue of living in this world among unrighteous men. What is important is that all experiences can be turned to our benefit.

We will struggle until we understand that all things have a purpose and will give us experience and learning. This learning is worth the pain that we suffer. We will struggle to trust God until we understand the truth with respect to the sin or trauma and see the blessings that have resulted from our suffering.

A child does not fully understand why his parent will let him struggle to learn how to swim. All the child sees is the parent backing away in the pool, stretching out the distance the child must swim, not saving him as quickly as he wants. Sometimes the child might feel terror when he first swallows a little water or when his parent first lets go. He does not understand why his parent, who always has helped and protected him before, is letting him sink. But the parent sees the bigger picture. The parent knows if she can teach the child to swim, she might prevent her child from drowning in the future. From the perspective of the parent, a little water in his nose is worth it. Just like children, we do not always understand why God allows painful things to happen, but we have to trust that, if we knew what he knew, it would make sense to us as well.

Fifth, negative emotions and thoughts can cause physical illness. Emotional healing may also allow physical healing to take place. The recognition and changing of negative beliefs and thought patterns, and the releasing of negative emotions, affect the physical functioning of our bodies. Disease may be just what it indicates: dis-ease.

I do not believe that all physical problems are cured through emotional healing alone. One must follow the direction of the spirit to see what else may be necessary and take additional steps if directed. For example, releasing negative emotions will not cure a broken leg, but it may speed the recovery. Also there might be chemical imbalances that require certain herbs or other treatments. I am saying that for long-term physical healing to take place, and to continue, we may need to address emotions as well as physical aspects.

The account of Zeezrom in the Book of Mormon provides an excellent example of the effect of negative emotions on the physical body. **"And also Zeezrom lay sick at Sidom, with a burning fever, which was caused by the great tribulations of his mind on account of his wickedness" (Alma 15:3).** Thoughts create either positive or negative emotions that in turn create healthy or unhealthy conditions in the body. It was not until he accepted the Atonement and found spiritual healing that his body was healed.

For many years I suffered through major and prolonged depression and felt as if I were dying. Each day I would feel as if my body was growing weaker and weaker, and when I would awake each morning it was difficult to move. My joints would swell and my general physical health continued to deteriorate. Once I understood the truth and moved through and released many of the negative emotions that caused the depression, I felt the flow of life energy come back into my body. My mind was enlightened and I began to feel a peace I had never experienced. Emotional healing is a process that helps us to be **"sanctified by the spirit unto the renewing of [our] bodies" (D&C 84:33).** We begin a process described in the scriptures as the "**sanctification of [our] hearts, which sanctification cometh because of [our] yielding [our] hearts unto God" (Helaman 3:35).** The spirit and light of Christ floods our soul as we recognize and work through negative thoughts and emotions and replace them with compassion.

A final reason we should heal emotionally is the effect that we have on others when we do not take care of our personal healing. As we discussed in Chapter 2, we often unintentionally take light and truth from others by the influence that we have in their lives.

As a parent, we instill the same fears and negative patterns of behavior in our children that we have struggled with all of our lives. Our children are like sponges, they do not shut out the negative comments or teasing that we may direct toward them. It quickly becomes a part of their subconscious, and they take on much of the same programming that we carry around in our own lives. Cell biologist, Dr. Bruce Lipton, states that, "Young children carefully observe their environment and download the worldly wisdom offered by parents directly into their subconscious memory. As a result, their parents' behavior and beliefs become their own."[4]

For example, a negative father never sees the positive in his child. He sees nothing but negative events and activities in his own environment. He always points out that the child is lacking in talent, intellect, and ability. He finds ways to criticize the child. The child considers himself to be stupid, a failure, incapable and can only see the negative. He may also seek to criticize others so that he can feel better about himself and soften his emotional pain. The cycle continues until someone recognizes and heals the emotions and works to replace the negative patterns.

A second example is a mother who has been sexually or physically abused as a child. She might withhold physical affection from her child because it makes her uncomfortable. It is difficult and hard for her to do. The child does not receive the amount of outward expressions of love and affection that humans need to be emotionally healthy and so he turns to worldly experiences and inappropriate outside attention looking for a replacement.

As a spouse, we may be reactionary, volatile, and many times unable to meet the needs of our partner because we are so needy ourselves. Our partner in marriage will be on the receiving end of our anger, negative comments, fears, and irrational behavior. For example, if one marriage partner has been through sexual abuse and the other has self-esteem problems, intimacy may be impossible. One may want nothing to do with intimacy while the other feels like the spouse does not care for them or desire them. Self-image declines and both are incapable of helping their spouse work through his or her problems.

Another example is a low self-esteem spouse with a co-dependant partner. At first, the spouse with low self-esteem may receive all the attention they are craving, but eventually they will tire of the clinginess. The co-dependent partner may become angry and frustrated because they are the one always giving and never receiving.

When both partners need to heal it can seem nearly impossible for them to make the marriage work. Unfortunately, a couple often receives counseling together to find ways to improve their relationship when the best thing might be for the individuals to first work through and heal some of their own issues. Then they can come together to learn better relationship principles and strategies to improve their marriage. A marriage counselor or bishop might suggest something impossible for the person to do at the time, such as asking an abuse or abandonment victim to be more affectionate. Even though more affection might be good for the marriage, the victim needs some healing before he or she will be able to follow this advice.

As a friend, emotional health will allow us to build healthy relationships and social ties. If we are not emotionally well, we drive others away from us by the irrational thoughts and actions we exhibit such as jealousy, being overly needy and demanding, invasion of personal space, constant focus on self, and control issues. One woman was abandoned by her mother as a child and has difficulty maintaining friendships with other women. She is always waiting for them to leave and constantly checking to make sure they are still her friends. She pushes them away by demanding too much of their time and maintenance.

I am sure there are additional reasons we need to heal, but the reasons listed above should stress how important it is to take action. Many of us are still functioning and see no need to make changes. There is not a person on earth that does not need emotional healing. Are we willing to seek solutions and discover the healing we need?

# WILLINGNESS TO HEAL

Everyone who suffers emotional trauma or pain from their own sins or the sins of others can be healed if they will. Everyone is entitled to God's help and the Savior's Atonement because "**God is no respecter of persons" (Acts 10:34)**. We are all equal in God's eyes.

The truth will only free us as much as we are willing to search it out, accept it, and apply it. Willingness implies humility and seeking at all costs. We must seek to be healed, not just ask, but seek. Seek means to search out information and learning, pray with all the energy of our heart for direction, and do what the spirit leads us to do, no matter what it is.

The questions we should ask ourselves are, "Am I willing to be healed? Am I willing to do whatever it takes to free myself of the pain and hurt? Am I worried about what it might be like if I were actually healed? Am I afraid to face life without an excuse? Do I get some satisfaction or find justification from my pain? Am I willing to face the fear that keeps me from taking action?"

We receive only that which we are willing to receive. The Lord revealed to the Prophet Joseph Smith, **"They shall return unto their own place, to enjoy that which they are willing to receive, because they were not willing to enjoy that which they might have received. For what doth it profit a man if a gift is bestowed upon him, and he receive not the gift"** (D&C 88:32,33). So much depends on our willingness to accept God's help. **"God [will] grant unto [us] that [our] burdens may be light, through the joy of his Son. And even all this can ye do if ye will"** (Alma 33:23). God will not give us his gifts if we are unwilling to receive them.

Pride is likely the greatest stumbling block keeping us from the healing power of the Atonement. It blocks our willingness to receive God's help. Pride is found among the wealthy and prominent down to the poorest beggar. We get a glimpse of how pride affects our willingness through a man named Amulek in the Book of Mormon. He tells us that he was, **"a man of no small reputation" (Alma 10:4).** Even though he was aware of the mysteries of God, he **"was called many times and [he] would not hear; therefore [he] knew concerning these things, yet [he] would not know; therefore [he] went on rebelling against God, in the wickedness of [his] heart" (Alma 10:6).** Amulek's reputation and possibly station and wealth made it difficult for him to follow the Lord, even when he knew the Lord was calling. He was unwilling and would not hear or know.

Another type of pride that affects our willingness occurs when we are **"at ease in Zion" (2 Nephi 28:24).** We may think, because we are fortunate enough to be a member of the church or a believer in Christ, we are safe, and we are much better off than those around us that do not appear to be religious or are choosing to participate in other religions. The stronger we hold to this belief the less willing we will be to move forward in humility. Jesus teaches us about this attitude with the following story from the New Testament. **"Two men went up into the temple to pray; the one a Pharisee, and the other a publican. The Pharisee stood and prayed thus with himself, God, I thank thee, that I am not as other men** *are,* **extortioners, unjust, adulterers, or even as this publican. I fast twice in the week, I give tithes of all that I possess. And the publican, standing afar off, would not lift up so much as** *his* **eyes unto heaven, but smote upon his breast, saying, God be merciful to me a sinner. I tell you, this man went down to his house justified** *rather* **than the other: for every one that exalteth himself shall be abased; and he that humbleth himself shall be exalted" (Luke 18:10-14).** Many members of the church go to the temple, pray, fast, and pay tithing. As we see, the Pharisee did the same. Let us consider what is in our heart when we worship and interact with others not of our belief. Our prayer should always be, "God be merciful to me a sinner." It is this humble attitude that will effectuate the atonement.

Another common manifestation of pride is reflected in an experience I had several years ago while visiting with an unwed pregnant mother of five children. Each child had a different father and the mother had never married. She was left to care for and provide the only support for herself and her children. She was destitute and struggling to care for her family. Although I could see she was in great emotional pain, she proceeded to blame the church, prior boyfriends, circumstances, God, and her family for her problems. I thought of the following scripture. **"Who am I, saith the Lord, that have promised and have not fulfilled? I command and men obey not; I revoke and they receive not the blessing. Then they say in their hearts: This is not the work of the Lord, for his promises are not fulfilled" (D&C 58:31-33).** She neither recognized nor accepted her responsibility for the painful consequences of her actions. She was in very humbling circumstances, but there was very little true humility in her heart, only pain. Her prideful attitude kept her from receiving the healing power of the Savior.

I do not imply that those who suffer have broken the commandments of God. Suffering is an important part of our existence on earth. We have a choice to make when trials are upon us. Whether our trials are consequences of poor choices or they are simply events beyond our control, the inclination to blame God and others for our difficulties increases with prolonged suffering.

The Lord told the early Apostles that they would face temptations and trials, and if they chose a humble attitude they would receive conversion and healing. **"And after their temptations, and much tribulation, behold, I, the Lord, will feel after them, and if they harden not** their hearts, and stiffen not their necks against me, they shall be converted, and I will heal them" (D&C 112:13). If we choose humility from our suffering, God promises that healing will come.

Some of us may believe that we have been knocked down and humbled so much that we could not possibly have any pride left in our hearts. Our perception of pride and the Lord's perception of pride may be very different. Living each day with emotional pain and being worn out from suffering are not synonymous with humility. Just because we feel we cannot lose any more dignity or cannot go on another day does not mean we are humble. Our experiences can and often will help us gain humility, but sometimes we fool ourselves. Some people just grow bitter as their suffering is prolonged. We have all known individuals who seem to be in constant suffering. To us it may appear that their suffering should be enough to produce humility, but when these people continue complaining or blaming others for their problems, they demonstrate that their suffering becomes an excuse instead of a tool to bring them to humility.

We manifest true humility by taking responsibility for our actions and by expressing gratitude without feeling shame. When Jesus met ten lepers, who cried for mercy, he told them to show themselves unto the priest, and **"as they went, they were cleansed."** Each of the lepers followed the counsel of Jesus and received physical healing. However, there was one leper in the group who **"turned back, and with a loud voice glorified God, and fell down on his face at his feet, giving him thanks" (Luke 17: 15-16).** All ten lepers acted upon the instructions given by the Savior to show themselves to the priest. All ten lepers were healed physically by following the Lord's directions. Because they acted they were blessed.

One leper understood his weakness in relation to God and turned back and gave thanks and received something more. The Savior said, **"Arise, go thy way: thy faith hath made thee whole " (Luke 17:19).** When Jesus states, **"Thy faith hath made thee whole,"** I do not believe that he is referring only to the physical healing that took place moments before. He seems to be declaring that the leper be healed in another way, perhaps spiritually and emotionally. The leper ignored what others thought of him as he fell on his face and expressed his gratitude in a loud voice. He was sincere and humble before God. True humility is displayed through a willingness to act and follow God while demonstrating our gratitude for the smallest blessings. True humility calls forth the power of the Atonement. It calls forth emotional and spiritual healing.

Sometimes we are not willing to heal because we gain a benefit from being a victim. We may tend to feel brave and courageous or even a step above others because we have dealt with such terrible circumstances. We may get something out of others' sympathy and their feeling sorry for us. This may be one way we get others to pay attention to us. Some people have one ailment or another that they are always complaining about to gain sympathy. Deep down they may be afraid of healing because they are afraid of losing that attention or possibly of losing the excuse for their behavior. They may also be afraid that others will not accept them for whom they really are if they let down their façades. This lifestyle results in complete emptiness and most people have no desire to be with someone who is seeking sympathy. It is a form of depending on the "arm of flesh" and not the arm of God. Emotional healing is a turning to God and a moving away from man.

We are the only ones that can make the choice to obtain healing. We allow pride, emotions, and irrational thoughts to rule and keep us in negative patterns and beliefs. It is only through our willingness and the grace of the Savior that our hearts begin to change. The following lines reflect the condition of so many of God's children.

### MIND'S PRISON

Our impudent, minds whirl madly,
Catalyst to every emotion.
In our self-made prison sadly,
We continue in pious devotion.
Unaware of the heavy doors.
Unaware of the ceilings and floors.
Locked in thoughts both future and past.
Key in hand yet holding fast.

Months, years, a lifetime passes.
Change will someday raise its accusing finger
Toward an inmate with darkened glasses.
Anger, fear, and hate need not linger.
Cut free all the roots that reach so deep.
Give 'way all the pain we feel to keep.
God changes hearts as we give place.
It is in His light that we find grace.

Many of us stay frozen, locked in our own self-made prison without moving forward, and yet we always have the key in our hand. We must be the first to act and unlock the door. The Savior is always ready when we are. If we choose to receive his healing, we will stop the cycle of passing on our irrational thoughts, false beliefs, and negative patterns to others.

There is no healing without a desire. Alma taught that acquiring faith, as well as any other spiritual gift, starts with our desire. **"But behold, if ye will awake and arouse your faculties, even to an experiment upon my words, and exercise a particle of faith, yea, even if ye can no more than desire to believe, let this desire work in you, even until ye believe in a manner that ye can give place for a portion of my words" (Alma 32:27).** If we are not willing to be healed, if we do not feel humility, we must pray for the desire. If we will pray for the desire to be healed and be diligent in our supplication, the desire will most assuredly come. God knows our hearts, and we need only be honest in our supplication.

Once we have the desire, we can be successful at change. **"Verily, verily, I say unto you, even as you desire of me so it shall be done unto you" (D&C 11:8).** We must be willing to receive the healing gift of the Savior by recognizing our level of humility, realizing that we are all sinners, and abandoning our will for God's will.

It is difficult to see life differently and to leave behind what is familiar to us for the unknown. It takes courage, effort, and desire. The one sure thing is that we must act to move forward spiritually.

# THE SAVIOR'S HEALING GRACE

Although emotional healing depends on our willingness, it is ultimately through the mercy and grace of the Savior that it occurs, **"for we know that it is by grace that we are saved; after all we can do" (2 Nephi 25:23). "But behold, he did deliver them because they did humble themselves before him; and because they cried mightily unto him he did deliver them out of bondage; and thus doth the Lord work with his power in all cases among the children of men; extending the arm of mercy towards them that put their trust in him" (Mosiah 29:20).** The Lord extends his arms of mercy in all cases.

I want to share two very personal experiences of great significance to me. Both events answered questions that I had been praying about and helped me better understand the importance of the Atonement in my life.

While struggling through severe depression, I found myself doubting what I had always thought to be true. One of my most pressing questions was whether or not Jesus Christ was literally the Savior of mankind. I believed that he had lived and done mighty things but I wanted to know if the Atonement was an actual event.

One morning, about 2:00 a.m., I awoke to a voice in my mind that said, "John 4:26." It was so clear and vivid that I sat upright in bed looking around to see who had spoken. I had no idea what this scripture was about. I found my scriptures and read the following verse: **"Jesus saith unto her, I that speak unto thee am he."** As I looked through the fourth chapter of John, I found that Jesus was responding to the statement of the Samaritan woman at the well. The woman said, **"I know that Messias cometh, which is called Christ: when he is come, he will tell us all things" (John 4:25).** In very few words he testified of his mission and divinity in his response to the woman. Through this verse, Jesus was telling me that he was the Messiah, the Savior of the world, which meant that I could indeed look to him for healing and salvation.

In my second experience, I had a dream that I was a drug addict living in a small town. I could feel what it was like to be unable to stop the addiction. I felt the pain that I caused everyone and the way it feels to be rejected by everyone you know. I could see the sadness and fear in their eyes. I was going from house to house trying to find someone who cared about me but no one would risk their friendship. They had been hurt too badly. I finally went into the middle of the main street and fell on my knees in despair, crying to God for help. At once, I began to sense that the Savior was coming to heal me. I knew it was the Savior but I could not see him clearly. He kept coming closer but I awoke moments before he arrived. I knew without question that his intent in coming was to heal me. **"And he shall cast out devils, or the evil spirits which dwell in the hearts of the children of men" (Mosiah 3:6).** When I awoke, I was overcome with the reality of his power to heal the heart. I realized that he was the only way to gain salvation and healing in this life and the world to come.

When we seek the Savior's help, we must be humble and plead with him to soften and heal our hearts. **"He healeth the broken in heart, and bindeth up their wounds" (Psalms 147:3).** The Lord promises to change our hearts when he says, **"A new heart also will I give you, and a new spirit will I put within you: and I will take away the stony heart out of your flesh, and I will give you an heart of flesh" (Ezekiel 36:26).** Jesus desires to give us a new heart fashioned after his own.

We see the Lord manifest his power to change hearts among the people in the writings of Alma. **"Behold, he changed their hearts; yea, he awakened them out of a deep sleep, and they awoke unto God... And according to his (Alma's) faith there was a mighty change wrought in his heart. And behold, he preached the word unto your fathers, and a mighty change was also wrought in their hearts, and they humbled themselves and put their trust in the true and living**

**God. And now behold, I ask of you, my brethren of the church, have ye spiritually been born of God? Have ye received his image in your countenances? Have ye experienced this mighty change in your hearts" (Alma 5:7,12-14).** It is certain that a change of heart is essential to salvation, and it always involves Christ. He is the one that produces the change according to our faith in him.

In George Richie's book, *Return From Tomorrow*, he tells of his near death experience while in the military. He recounts the appearance of a glorious being at his side that tells him that he is Jesus. Jesus communicates to Richie's mind, "Keep your eyes on me." At once they begin an incredible journey where George Richie sees many amazing and wonderful things. At times he feels terror and sadness, but he finds that, each time he looks back at Christ, peace returns to him.[5]

It is the same for each of us as we seek healing here in mortality. **"Thou wilt keep him in perfect peace, whose mind is stayed on Thee" (Isaiah 26:3).** If we will stay focused on Christ and keep our eyes and mind on him, we will obtain and retain peace in our lives.

In Numbers, Chapter 21, the children of Israel complained and spoke against God. Because of their ingratitude and disrespect, fiery serpents came and many people were bitten and died. When the people repented, Moses was told by God to make a serpent out of brass and to put it on a pole. Anyone who had been bitten by a serpent could look at the brass serpent and be healed. Many would not look because they did not believe this could heal them. The people that did look were healed. This experience was a type and representation of the

Savior. He tells us that if we will but look to him we can be healed.

We may ask ourselves the question, how do we look to Christ? He tells us **"Look unto me in every thought; doubt not, fear not" (D&C 6:36).** He tells us to look to him by controlling and focusing our actions and thoughts upon his example, his teachings, his blessings, his sacrifice, and his great love for us. If we do so, he offers us the same blessings he offered the people of Moses.

Jesus speaks to us with encouraging words. He wants us to understand that he is the door to healing and peace. He said to Martha, **"I am the resurrection, and the life; he that believeth in me, though he were dead, yet shall he live" (John 11:25).** He told the Apostle Thomas, **"I am the way, the truth and the life; no man cometh unto the father but by me" (John 14:6).** If we have been bitten by abuse, heartache, sin, depression or any other hurtful or painful experience, we can look to the Savior with humility and prayer, and he can heal our pain. **"Yea, cry unto him for mercy; for he is mighty to save. Yea, humble yourselves, and continue in prayer unto him" (Alma 34:18-19).** Christ makes emotional and spiritual healing possible.

Do not give up when it seems like God does not hear you. He does hear you and will help you. I spent so many years ignoring that something was wrong and many more years trying to figure it out, all the while not realizing that God was preparing me and preparing the way so I could accept his help and healing. For most, like myself, it takes time to heal. For others, the Savior can take away the spiritual and emotional pain we are experiencing right now, this very moment. **"If ye will repent and harden not your hearts, <u>immediately</u> shall the great plan of redemption be brought about unto you" (Alma 34: 31).** We do not always need to wait for years to have relief from our pain. What I want to emphasize is that when we are prepared to receive it, the change can happen rapidly. I said it took me many years, but actually, when I was sufficiently humble and ready, it came very fast, almost instantaneously. It is just that it took me many years to be humble and ready, and it is taking many more years to instill the changes and recognized truths as a permanent part of my soul.

Jeffery R Holland of the Quorum of the Twelve Apostles said, "You can change anything you want to change and you can do it very fast. That's another satanic sucker-punch --- that it takes years and years and eons of eternity to repent. It takes exactly as long to repent as it takes you to say I'll change --- and mean it. Of course there will be problems to work out and restitutions to make. You may well spend --- indeed you had better spend --- the rest of your life proving your repentance by its permanence. But change, growth, renewal, repentance can come for you as instantaneously as it did for Alma and the Sons of Mosiah."[6]

Gaining emotional healing and forgiveness through the Savior may be immediate, but recognizing negative patterns and false beliefs may take some time. The advantage will be that once our heart begins to change we are working on addictions and problems from a stronger position, one of increased love and acceptance for ourselves and for the Lord.

The healing grace of Jesus Christ is only effective for those who make the effort. To better understand this concept, the following story may be of help. As an advisor in a teacher's quorum, I took our teachers to the south rim of the Grand Canyon on a fishing trip. We hiked for four hours, and when we arrived we could see that there was a waterfall on the other side of a steep cliff wall from our camping area. One afternoon a young man and I were near the wall, and he challenged me to go across it and see the waterfalls. Observing the wall, I could see a tiny ledge about one inch wide where I could put the toes of my shoes. I also noticed a long clothesline hanging from a very small bush protruding from the wall of the cliff about 25 feet up. I do not know how it got there, but I assumed that I could make it with the help of this small cord. I wrapped it around my hand and started out. The Colorado River was rushing below my feet as I moved along the edge. I soon found that the ledge was wet and covered with slick moss. When I reached about halfway, I fell from the ledge and found myself hanging by one hand from this tiny cord with my feet dangling in the turbulent rushing water.

I knew that my only way out of this situation was the cord and my own efforts to pull myself up. There was no way for someone else to help me. I eventually pulled myself up and worked my way back to the beginning with a grateful heart that my experience was not fatal.

This experience allows me to make the following comparison. I imagine the cord to represent the grace and outstretched hand of the Savior through his atonement and the water to represent the temptations, evils, and dangers of this world. We are all spiritually dangling dangerously over prideful attitudes, addictions, complacency, bitterness, selfishness, and other sins while the grace of the Savior is mercifully extended to us. **"And thus mercy can satisfy the demands of justice, and encircles them in the arms of safety"** (Alma 34:16). Most of the time, we probably do not even realize the full extent of our condition.

We can choose at any moment in our lives to let go and move away from the Savior's grace and be swept into perilous waters or to make efforts to pull ourselves up and out by deliberately seeking the Savior. The fact is that even with the grace of Jesus Christ extended in mercy, we must do, we must act, and we must make efforts or we will not gain healing. Let it be clear that our efforts do not pay for our sins, the Savior does. Our efforts allow us to take advantage of the changing power of the Atonement.

Let me offer a few words of caution. Many individuals who have been controlled by others through some form of abuse or trauma, feel a strong need to be in control of their lives and future. This is a perfectly natural response because of the painful results of being under another person's control. Control is especially important when it relates to physical safety. It has been difficult for me to not be the one flying the plane or driving the car. This control also applies to spiritual things. We think we must completely count on ourselves to obtain the blessings of the Lord. We not only want to control our obedience but also the blessings we will receive. We find that it is very difficult for us to rely on someone else for our salvation, including the Savior.

There is a fine balance between our trust and reliance on the Atonement and the efforts we should be making to do our part. As mentioned at the beginning of this chapter, Nephi teaches, **"for we know that it is by grace that we are saved, after all we can do" (2 Nephi 25:23).** Let us be careful not to fall into the trap of depending too heavily upon the arm of flesh due to our need to have control. We should continue to work out our salvation but turn over the control to Jesus Christ.

There is an additional danger in depending on our efforts alone without the Savior's mercy. We are not just fighting against the physical realities around us, but we are working daily against a host of unseen beings that want us to remain in a hopeless condition. **"For we wrestle not against flesh and blood, but against principalities, against powers, against the rulers of the darkness of the world, against spiritual wickedness in high places…" (Eph 6:12).** There is much opposition from the other side of the veil. **"Wherefore, [Satan] maketh war with the saints of God, and encompasseth them round_about" (D&C 76:29).** Satan and his followers are real, and they seek to overthrow all that is good and positive. He desires to negate and minimize the importance of the Atonement. We often do not see that Satan and his followers encourage us in our personal weaknesses. They desire our destruction. The following scriptures give very accurate descriptions of Satan and his character. **"Be sober, be vigilant, because your adversary the devil,**

**as a roaring lion, walketh about, seeking whom he may devour" (1 Peter 5:8). "And he beheld Satan; and he had a great chain in his hand; and it veiled the whole face of the earth with darkness, and he looked up and laughed, and his angels rejoiced" (Moses 7:26).** Satan will gain even greater power over our souls if we do not seek the protection and healing influence of the Savior.

While serving as a bishop, I had a disturbing dream with a very direct message. I dreamed I was walking through the neighborhood where my ward members lived. I had the ability to see into each home and see the occupants. I noticed that there were strangers gathered around each family member. These strangers were constantly whispering into the ears of each individual. Some of the people were agitated, and one person came out of his home and confronted me with anger and hate. As I continued walking, I noticed that these strangers were in the homes of many members. I wondered who these people were. I soon found that a young stranger was fast approaching. As she walked up to me, she became a fearsome demon and rose up in my face ready to attack. I immediately realized that the strangers I had seen whispering in the ears of the church members were servants of Satan, waging a full assault on those that had made covenants with the Lord. I awoke almost completely overwhelmed with the magnitude of Satan's efforts and his evil power.

The following scripture verifies just how accurate this dream really was. **"And behold, others [Satan] flattereth away, and telleth them there is no hell; and**

he saith unto them: I am no devil, for there is none—
and thus he whispereth in their ears, until he grasps
them with his awful chains, from whence there is no
deliverance" (2 Nephi 28:22). I am convinced that Satan
and his followers are ever seeking to whisper lies into our
ears. What many of us do not realize is that when we are
struggling with guilt, loneliness, addictions, and other
weaknesses, Satan's followers are right there beside us
convincing us that we are not worthy and incapable of
being successful in our efforts.

So what can we do to overcome and protect
ourselves? "And they overcame him by the blood of
the Lamb, and by the word of their testimony" (Rev
12:11) We learn from this scripture that we overcome
Satan by applying and experiencing the power and grace
of the Atonement in our lives and confessing Christ
openly. The Lord also provides additional counsel to help
us withstand the adversary. "Verily, verily, I say unto
you, ye must watch and pray always, lest ye be
tempted by the devil, and ye be led away captive by
him. ... Behold, verily, verily, I say unto you, ye must
watch and pray always lest ye enter into temptation;
for Satan desireth to have you, that he may sift you as
wheat. Therefore ye must always pray unto the Father
in my name" (3 Nephi 18:15,18-19). God tells us that we
should pray always in Jesus name. Prayer must be in the
name of Christ because he is our mediator with the
Father. By praying in his name, we activate his grace and
power to provide us with his blessings. "Pray always, that
you may come off conqueror; yea, that you may
conquer Satan, and that you may escape the hands of

the servants of Satan that do uphold his work" **(D&C 10:5).** By seeking the grace of God through prayer and faith, we push these evil influences away so that we can hear and understand the pure voice of the Holy Ghost. If we are always praying it will be much easier to look unto Christ in every thought.

Christ did not come to condemn us; he came to provide an example and a way to overcome the demands of justice. Were it not for his Atonement, our experiences and trials on earth would be meaningless.

Ponder his words and allow them to sink deep into your heart as he pleads with the Father for you and me. **"Listen to him who is the advocate with the Father, who is pleading your cause before him— Saying: Father, behold the sufferings and death of him who did no sin, in whom thou wast well pleased; behold the blood of thy Son which was shed, the blood of him whom thou gavest that thyself might be glorified; Wherefore, Father, spare these my brethren that believe on my name, that they may come unto me and have everlasting life**. **(D&C 45:3-5)**

Christ is pleading for us before the Father, but the interesting thing is that he is not presenting our good works and efforts before the Father. Christ is presenting his works, his sacrifice and his Atonement before the Father. He is asking the Father to accept his efforts on our behalf. He is asking us to believe on his name and exercise our faith through obedience, and his **"bowels of mercy; [will be] filled with compassion towards the children of men; [he will stand] betwixt them and justice" (Mosiah 15:9).**

Because justice must be satisfied, Christ will stand between each of us and the Father, presenting himself and his sacrifice to meet all of the demands of justice so that we might be saved in the kingdom of the Father through his great mercy. Through our obedience and faith in Christ we show our gratitude to him for his sacrifice and we free Christ's atoning power so that his intercession will meet the demands of justice for us individually.

Imagine for a moment how God must feel having sacrificed his eldest son so that all of his children could be redeemed. So many people ignore his infinite and eternal sacrifice. **"And then shall they know that I am the Lord their God, that I am their Redeemer; but they would not be redeemed" (Mosiah 26:26).** Even those of us who consider ourselves faithful and good people, often ignore the grace of God by believing that we must do everything ourselves or by not turning over our bitterness to Christ. We think that our salvation depends entirely on us. No matter how hard we strive to be good and keep the commandments it is impossible to be redeemed without the grace of the Atonement. Our daily repentance, obedience, faith, and good works are also required so that **"by his grace ye may be perfect in Christ"** and **"that ye become holy without spot" (Moroni 10:32,33).** It is by our obedience to God's laws that we, through the changing power of grace, become like God and are able to live again in his presence. It is the only way to become perfected.

I return again to the parable of the Pharisee and the publican referred to in Chapter 4. **"And the publican, standing afar off, would not lift up so much as *his*** eyes unto heaven, but smote upon his breast, saying, God be merciful to me a sinner." It demonstrates the attitude required by each of us as we go before the Father each day in prayer seeking His mercy. If we follow the publican's example to seek the Lord's mercy by pleading before God each day, the spirit of God will come upon us, and the Atonement will come to life in our hearts and in our minds. We will experience the change in our hearts that will bring about a new life. If we understand that we are all sinners in need of God's grace, we can be washed clean in the blood of the Lamb every single day. It now makes perfect sense to me why the scriptures tell us that, **"no unclean thing can enter into his kingdom; therefore nothing entereth into his rest save it be those who have washed their garments in my blood, because of their faith, and the repentance of all their sins, and their faithfulness unto the end" (3 Nephi 27:19).** If we apply the Atonement of Christ every day of our lives and strive to keep the commandments, we will be made clean and Christ will intercede before the Father.

Remember that we are all going to make mistakes, and often we will repeat the same offenses. God will forgive us of these offenses if we are continually striving to overcome them. Changes take time and effort, and sometimes reoccurrences take place. We should not get down on ourselves. Just keep getting up and going to the Father seeking the Savior's grace. He will forgive and your heart will change. Through this merciful process you will become perfected in Christ.

# THE LOVE OF GOD

Experiencing the pure love of Christ is the natural result of emotional healing, and true emotional healing occurs through the Atonement. It is often referred to as being born again. As we experience God, we experience his love because that is his nature. **"Beloved let us love one another; for love is of God; and everyone that loveth is born of God, and knoweth God. He that loveth not knoweth not God; for God is love" (1 John 4:7-8).** We can know that we are in a place of forgiveness toward self and others when we feel God's love. Being born of God is not just a one-time experience but can and should be experienced over and over. Each time we change anger and hate to compassion, we are reborn a little more in the likeness of God.

Jesus taught the people, **"Except a man be born again, he cannot see the kingdom of God" (John 3:3).** If the darkness is not removed from our eyes, we will not be able to see the Kingdom of God or enjoy the love of

God in our hearts. When negative emotions are released, the darkness dissipates and the light of Christ illuminates our soul.

As Lehi and his family press forward, holding to the rod of iron as recorded in 1 Nephi 8, Lehi sees a beautiful tree and fruit that is most delicious. We discover in chapter 11 that the tree represents the love of God, and that **"it is most desirable above all things…Yea, and the most joyous to the soul" (1 Nephi 11:22-23).** The scriptures do not tell us directly what the fruit represents. They do, however, describe the beauty and feeling that comes from partaking of the fruit by saying; **"the fruit was desirable to make one happy…it was most sweet, above all that I ever before tasted…the fruit thereof was white, to exceed all the whiteness that I had ever seen. And as I partook of the fruit thereof it filled my soul with exceedingly great joy" (1 Nephi 8:10-12).** I had always believed the fruit also represented the love of God based on this scriptural account of the joy associated with the fruit.

Shortly after entering the mission field, my son wrote me a letter and observed that he believed the fruit represented the Atonement. It made perfect sense to me considering the Atonement would be the ultimate demonstration of love, and partaking of the Atonement would bring about the feelings described in these verses. An act only so entirely selfless as the Atonement could produce a feeling of gratitude and love so intense in nature that it could motivate a man to give all that he is to God.

Notice that the reward or the fruit for being faithful and holding to the rod of iron is not great material wealth or things that we touch or hold. It is a feeling, an emotion. Material things will never bring lasting happiness and joy. Everyone knows there are many miserable wealthy and popular people. We often read in the news of their addictions, aberrant behavior, and divorces. They appear on countless talk shows discussing how to be happy but never arrive at a solution. According to the scriptures, the fruit of the tree **"is the greatest of all the gifts of God" (1Nephi 15:36).** The love of God is a powerful feeling. The words used in the scriptures to describe God's love are most desirable and most joyous to the soul. Who are we willing to forgive and what sins are we willing to repent of in exchange for this remarkable feeling?

I came to understand the importance of the love of God while working as a program manager for a residential treatment center for juvenile delinquents. I became very frustrated as I continually watched these at-risk youth go through detention and treatment centers like ours and end up in the adult prison system after being released into the public at age 18. It usually took no time at all for them to be arrested again. As I struggled over this, I prayed that I might know what I could do to help these kids change their lives.

One night I had a dream that answered my question. In my dream, I was a guard in an adult prison facility. There was one inmate that was very different from the rest. He was extremely disgusting and his face was covered with slime and filth. He was large and powerful and filled with hate and anger. He was contained in a small fenced area with several guards assigned to keep him locked up. I was one of the guards assigned to watch him. Every few minutes, he would break the gate open and run, and we would chase him and wrestle him back into the pen and lock the gate again. After we had done this many times, he broke out again and I found myself chasing him by myself. I caught up to him and tackled him with my arms locked around his body and my face up against his face.

We went down hard, and I could feel the intense anger and tension in his body as I tried to hold him down. All at once, an indescribable power of love and compassion enveloped the two of us. It was just as the scriptures describe the love of God. It filled my soul with exceedingly great joy and peace. I felt the tension release in this man I was holding down. I instinctively knew that he was enveloped in this power as well. I released my grip and got to my feet. As he stood up, his face was completely clear and radiant, his anger and hate were gone. He stood quietly basking in the love of God. He was completely healed. I awoke with this wonderful feeling still lingering. I could see that the love of God was the greatest life changing power in the world. I also knew that I needed this power in my life if I were to really make a difference in the lives of others.

The love of God is an emotion so positive and joyous that we think and feel as stated in the New Testament. **"Charity (the love of God) suffereth long, and is kind; charity envieth not; charity vaunteth not itself, is not puffed up, Doth not behave itself unseemly, seeketh not her own, is not easily**

**provoked, thinketh no evil; Rejoiceth not in iniquity, but rejoiceth in the truth; Beareth all things, believeth all things, hopeth all things, endureth all things. Charity never faileth" (1 Corinthians 13:4-8).** It is easy to see that, when we have not healed our negative emotions, we cannot love self or others. We continually focus on our needs. In this condition, we cannot feel the characteristics of charity mentioned above. We seek our own (never have enough, focused on self, look out only for our interest, must have control), we are puffed up (prideful, a need to elevate ourselves above others, compare our situations), filled with envy (never being satisfied or having enough), unkind, easily provoked (impatient, angry, abusive), rejoice in iniquity, (find pleasure in the misfortunes and failure of others), behave unseemly (struggle with sinful actions), and have trouble believing and enduring. We find that we are far from the love spoken of in the scriptures.

Over the first twenty years of our marriage, my wife and I taught our children the value of obedience, but we did not understand the importance of allowing them the opportunity to express their emotions and feelings. In reality, there are few families that validate the feelings of their children. To validate feelings means to accept feelings as genuine and verbally recognize feelings as real or valid. Our lack of understanding resulted in our children holding in most of their negative as well as positive emotions. Once we realized our mistake, we called a meeting and gathered the children together. We set guidelines allowing each of us to maintain respect for one another, and we gave each child the opportunity to express his or her feelings about some very difficult circumstances that had transpired in our family over the previous few years. It turned out to be a very spiritual experience. We saw a positive change in the personalities of the children. They began to feel safe expressing their feelings. This allowed them the opportunity to get things out in the open and work through them. They each seemed to be empowered in their interactions with others.

My daughter later recounted that, after this experience, she naturally had a desire to turn her attention outward to others instead of focusing on her own problems as she usually did. When we gathered at her grandmother's home right after our family meeting, she found herself asking others about themselves and being concerned for them. She had always forced herself to reach out before. She said it felt like previously trapped energy had been freed up inside her, and now she could use it. Obviously, she had moved some negative emotions out that had plagued her for some time and the light of Christ had been magnified in her heart.

When we are filled with the love of God, we have a natural inclination to do the will of God and bless his children, **"For he that loveth another hath fulfilled the law... Love worketh no ill to his neighbour: therefore love is the fulfilling of the law" (Romans 13:8,10).** Keeping the commandments will become easy because we will choose goodness.

The scriptures reveal two additional keys that will bring the love of God into our souls. The Lord encourages us to **"Pray unto the Father with all the energy of heart, that ye may be filled with this love" (Moroni**

7:48). He also urges us to **"bridle all your passions, that ye may be filled with love" (Alma 38:12).** We must ask specifically for the gift of his love through sincere prayer, and we should control our passions and appetites so that we might be pure vessels to receive his light and love.

# GUILT

The purpose of guilt is to bring us to repentance and change. Once we are motivated to action it is important that we turn our guilt over to the Savior.

Guilt becomes unhealthy when we feel so unworthy that we become immobilized by our feelings of low self worth. Many members of the church confess and refrain from sin but continue to feel unworthy or guilty. Other members live near perfect lives, but feel unworthy because of the few weaknesses they do have. They continue to feel this way because they are not and cannot be perfect. These feelings incapacitate and distract many good people, keeping them from having confidence, serving others, and doing God's will.

Many parents struggle with guilt because they blame themselves when their children choose to use drugs, question their testimony, forego serving a mission or select an alternative lifestyle. They forget that their children came to earth with a unique personality and the ability and freedom to choose. They must also remember that they have been learning to parent, and at the same time, deal with their own emotions, testimony, relationships, trials, and responsibilities.

Both good and bad parents have struggled with problem children. If we dwell on what we should have done, the guilt and fear will completely immobilize us, and we will be of no help to our children in the future. God struggled with his children; we may struggle with ours. In the Bible, Job understood the power of fear when he lamented, **"For the thing which I greatly feared is come upon me, and that which I was afraid of is come unto me" (Job 3:25).** Fearing that we or our loved ones will not make it to heaven, takes us away from the feelings of love required to help others move toward God.

God understands this and teaches us the antidote for fear. **"There is no fear in love; but perfect love casteth out fear: because fear hath torment. He that feareth is not made perfect in love" (1 John 4:18).** If we feel the love of God in our hearts as we discussed in Chapter 6, we will cease to operate from a position of fear.

Sometimes we may feel guilt for things that are no fault of our own. When we are emotionally traumatized through something like sexual abuse or abandonment, we often feel responsible for the actions perpetrators have committed against us. We take responsibility for others' violent or hurtful actions, thinking that we caused them by something we must have done or said, or by being somewhere we should not have been. It is important to recognize the difference between being a victim and being responsible for our actions. Anytime a child is abused or forced by an adult or an older child, the younger child is a victim, even if the child allowed it to happen or may have derived some pleasure from the experience. A child does not really understand the implications or the ramifications associated with the abuse. If an adult is forced or harmed in any way by another adult, he or she is also a victim.

As a victim of abuse or trauma, we have not sinned, we are not guilty, and we are not responsible for the event or actions of others in any way. We are the victims of another person's sin. It is irrational to think that we should be blamed for another person's actions. However, if we perpetuate the abuse on others in the future or if we fail to forgive, we will then be held accountable.

We also feel guilt as we formulate judgments and compare ourselves to others. How many times have we been in a church meeting looking around at all the perfect people and perfect families? If we only knew the struggles that each person has in his or her life, we would not spend our time comparing. Every person has his **"thorn in the flesh"** as the Apostle Paul described it, something that he or she struggles with every day **(2 Corinthians 12:7).** Feeling guilty for not being perfect or for not being as righteous as we think others may be is a poor motivator. Comparing ourselves to, or thinking we need to be as good or better than someone else, always creates more guilt than is necessary. Others generally appear better than they are. We will never be able to live up to these imaginary standards we set as we compare.

Some years ago my wife and I attended the Chandler, Arizona Rotary track meet. We were there from early morning until late at night watching our son pole vault. The last event of the night was the 3200-meter run (approx. two miles). I happened to be sitting next to a gentleman whose daughter would be running in the race. He pointed her out to me with pride. As the race progressed, I watched her slowly drop behind many of the other 60 runners from the 30 schools involved in this meet. By the time she crossed the finished line, she was about 6th from last place. I assumed she would be discouraged with her performance.

As the bleachers cleared, she bounded up toward us with a huge smile on her face. Filled with excitement she blurted out, "Dad, I beat my personal best by 20 seconds." I was amazed at her attitude. She was not comparing herself to others but only to herself and the best she could do. There was no shame or guilt in her soul because she knew she was doing her best.

We should only seek to do our personal best. If we continually compare ourselves to others' accomplishments, all that we do will be out of fear that we will not measure up, and we will never be or feel good enough. When we keep the commandments out of fear and guilt, we begin to resent the gospel and blame the church for not making us feel better. We see the Gospel as a set of rules designed to make life more difficult. We need to understand that everyone is imperfect. There are no perfect people. Sometimes the little bit that we do may be the best that we can do at the time. If we could do better, it is possible we would be doing better. If we could exhibit more faith at the moment, it is possible that we would. It usually takes time and learning to arrive at certain levels of devotion and obedience.

There was a time in my own life when I was in complete despair. Everything I did was based on guilt and fear, worried that my actions were never enough to please God. I knew that my way of thinking was not bringing me joy and happiness and that something was terribly wrong. I had to start over and rethink my belief system. I put all of my beliefs up on a spiritual clothesline and took them down one by one to examine them. I started with God and asked myself, "What kind of a God have I been trying to worship?" Once I realized I worshiped a severe God, I decided that it did not make sense to seek a God of wrath. If I was overwhelmed and fearful of my outcome, I was thinking of the wrong heaven anyway. I was really concentrating on hell, not on heaven. Once I recognized that my thinking was irrational, I wanted to find what God was really like. As I reflected and prayed, I determined that the God I really desired to worship was a God that loves me despite my failings and works with me to help me grow to be just like him. This was a God that made sense. As I continued my quest, I came to know for myself that God's nature really is love.

If we consider our own children, at what point do we say we are through loving them? How far will we go to provide for and protect them? Are we not always willing to nurture them when they are trying to progress? If our child has been involved in drugs, do we not reach out to help her when she is trying to change? If she is destructive and not willing to try, we may send her away, but as long as she is trying, we will do our all to help her. It makes sense that God would do the same. I realized that if I was trying, God would help me move forward.

Although we should have God-given sorrow for addictions, pornography or other indiscretions, guilt and shame can play a huge role in keeping us from overcoming the sin. When we first decide to repent, we have enthusiasm and a desire to never commit the sin again. When we slip or fall, we start with negative self-talk such as; "I have already fallen, I might as well keep doing it; I am a failure; I will never get over this addiction; I am a bad person; I will never change; I am just a loser; I might as well not try."

With these thoughts in mind, we feel worse and worse about ourselves and lose the drive to fight back. The "why try" attitude gives us permission to keep sinning. Satan's greatest tool is to make us think we are lost and can never change. The most important thing is to get back up when we fall. Relapses and reoccurrences are often part of the journey to healing.

Remember, healing emotions does not automatically take away our negative patterns of behavior; it changes the way we look at these patterns so that we can accept and work on them. It allows the light of Christ and the Holy Ghost to give us added strength and clarity of thought, and it fills a need that we have been seeking to fill elsewhere. We still must focus on the details of change through replacement of negative patterns and false beliefs. Many of us have been acting a certain way for a very long time. If we have viewed pornography for many years, even though we will be seeing and feeling with a clearer understanding, we will still need to work to overcome the regular habit and the intense psychological and physiological rush that keeps us trapped in the addiction. If we have been negative all of our lives, it will take effort on our part to succeed at being positive.

We must take credit for the minutes, hours, and days we are successful at changing negative patterns. Let us recognize the situations that take us back to sin and stay with a focused plan. Avoid negative self-talk, it will only serve to take us deeper into the darkness. We are all children of God and equal in his sight. He loves us all, and we are all entitled to his healing power. No matter how many times we fail, he will pick us up, forgive us, and still love us. We should never give up. Let us remember that, as long as we are trying, he can help.

Let guilt be an emotion that moves us toward the Savior and positive action. If we repent and continue to feel guilt for our sins, we have not truly experienced the Atonement at work in our lives. We may think our sins are too great to be forgiven, but consider this verse in the Book of Mormon referring to a people who converted to God. **"And also He hath forgiven us of these our many sins and murders which we have committed, and taken away the guilt from our hearts, through the merits of his Son "** (Alma 24:10). These people had committed murders and great sins, but the Lord still extended his grace and the Atonement in their behalf and took away their guilt.

Enos teaches us how to receive the blessings of forgiveness and be relieved of our guilt. **"My soul hungered; and I kneeled down before my Maker, and I cried unto him in mighty prayer and supplication for mine own soul; and all the day long did I cry unto him; yea, and when the night came I did still raise my voice** high that it reached the heavens. **And there came a voice unto me, saying: Enos, thy sins are forgiven thee, and thou shalt be blessed. And I, Enos, knew that God could not lie; wherefore, my guilt was swept away. And I said: Lord, how is it done? And he said unto me: Because of thy faith in Christ, whom thou hast never before heard nor seen" (Enos 1:3-8).** This account teaches us an important formula. First, hunger for forgiveness; second, humbly cry unto the Lord in prayer; and third, do not be willing to go away empty. Continue with persistence until the Lord grants your petition. It may not be necessary that you stay up all night in prayer but be consistent in your daily supplications. God will hear you.

# SUFFERING

Many ask why there is so much suffering, especially those who have endured extreme abuses. Why does God not do something about the innocent suffering that takes place every day? Many people are killed or incapacitated for the extent of their mortal journey by acts of violence or other unforeseen occurrences. Some people are born with debilitating illnesses or deformities. Why does God allow some of us to be hurt at an age when we could not protect ourselves? This is an extremely big issue, especially if we have pain and hurt that we are dealing with every day of our lives.

We may find that it is difficult, if not impossible, to have faith and trust in a God that would allow suffering to occur. Many people who suffer from abuse or trials have lost faith and trust in God. They blame him and feel anger for their misfortunes. They say in their hearts, "How could he let this happen? Why didn't he protect me?"

My oldest daughter was ready to begin her second year of college and was invited to go skiing at a nearby lake with a group of friends close to her age. One of the young men was driving the boat while my daughter and another girl were riding on a tube behind the boat. The boat was pulling them through a narrow canyon, and the young man failed to follow the rules of safety by going through the canyon on the left side of the channel instead of the right. He could not see any oncoming boats, and as he rounded the corner another boat came around from the other direction. He turned to get out of the way of the oncoming boat, thereby throwing the two girls directly in the path of the other boat. The boat knocked the other girl free of the tube with minor injuries. It ran over my daughter and the tube. She was upside down when the boat prop hit her, breaking a leg and an arm, leaving deep gashes on both of her legs.

She was pulled up on the other boat and taken to shore where she was picked up 45 minutes later by an air evacuation medical helicopter. It was at this time that she first received something for her pain. She described to me the unbearable pain. She could not understand how God could allow someone to hurt so badly and endure so much pain. A year later, she realized that ever since the accident she felt her prayers did not seem to get past the ceiling. The accident had created for her a difficulty in trusting the Lord. She thought, "If God could allow this to happen to me, what else might he allow to happen? How can I have confidence that he will protect me from other terrible experiences?"

When we have these thoughts and feelings, we begin to build a wall of fear and doubt, driving out true faith. The faith that God wants us to have is not that he will keep bad things from happening to us; it is the faith that whatever happens to us, he will be part of it, be there for us, and he will help us through it. It is the faith that we will be more like him because of our experiences, and we will learn something important for our progress.

We may not understand some of the reasons for specific events until this life is ended. In my daughter's case, it may be possible that one of the youth riding in the boat that day may choose to take a specific precaution on a future boat outing that may save someone else from an untimely death. It may be that the accident allowed my daughter to begin to have doubts necessary for her to seek God more diligently to find answers. This accident is one of those opportunities to seek personal truth that may change perspective about the event, build spiritual maturity, and thus win her heart to God.

Acquiring faith may be one of the greatest hurdles we will need to overcome and the most important. So many of our experiences influence our faith in God. As a child, if a parent's example is abusive, unkind or nonexistent because of death, divorce, or preoccupation, it is difficult to see God as someone who loves and cares about us. This is because children often develop their image of God by the parenting figures in their lives. In a professional study, "Psychologists compared the words adults used to describe their childhood recollections of their parents with their current perceptions of God. Those with the most negative image of their parents had the most negative image of God."[7] This may seem unfair, but we must remember that our situations are specially suited to our growth and learning.

God's love is complete and perfect. He does care about his children. If God were to take away our suffering and obstacles, we would be left weak and dependent instead of gaining strength and confidence. If God relieved all of the suffering on the earth, this earthly existence would be meaningless. It would undermine man's agency and curtail our development. It is much like the principles behind bodybuilding. Muscles require resistance to grow and develop. The muscles are torn down to become stronger. Just as a bodybuilder, we face resistance and are knocked down to gain strength.

God must also allow people to act and to choose. He tells us specifically that he is not the author of the evil things that occur in life. **"The Lord God hath commanded that men should not murder; that they should not lie; that they should not steal; that they should not take the name of the Lord their God in vain; that they should not envy; that they should not have malice; that they should not contend one with another; that they should not commit whoredoms; and that they should do none of these things; for whoso doeth them shall perish. For none of these iniquities come of the Lord; for he doeth that which is good among the children of men" (2 Nephi 26:32-33).** God lets his children make their choices and those choices will affect other people.

Often, those that are affected by these bad choices are left with much scarring and hurt. God knew this would occur. He allows us to suffer trials to shape and mold our soul and teach us how to apply the Atonement. The negative emotions that result from trials and abuses encourage us to search out and apply the Atonement and come to understand the love that the Savior has for us and for those that have offended us. This allows us to have compassion and love for all people. If we have suffered through and conquered addictions, we feel compassion for, and are in a position to help, others with the same problems. We know exactly what it is like. Paul understood this in his comments to the Corinthians. He says that God **"comforteth us in all our tribulation, that we may be able to comfort them which are in any trouble, by the comfort wherewith we ourselves are comforted of God" (2 Corinthians 1: 4).** When we experience the comfort and healing power of God, we are in a position to help others acquire this experience in their own lives.

We must search and ask God what lessons we are to learn from every difficult experience. We can be sure there is a lesson, and if we do not discover and learn from it, we may often continue to repeat similar experiences until we do. Sometimes there is a reason a woman will marry three or four abusive husbands in a row. There is something about the way she views herself and others that may be irrational and unhealthy and may draw these circumstances into her life. These situations force her to analyze with great introspection, if she will, and seek truth and the healing power of the Lord.

After many years I realized the value of some of my childhood suffering. It has helped me recognize those who have suffered similar experiences and made me sensitive to their needs. It has also pushed me in a quest to seek diligently to know more about my relationship with God and his role in healing. There are many blessings that have come from my childhood abuse.

Another consideration is that some of these adverse situations are not as much for the individuals with the handicap, trial, infirmity, or the one taken in death, but for those required to care for them or live without them. We can all learn from the suffering of others. It is moving to watch as people struggle with trials and do so with an attitude of gratitude and faith. It lifts our soul and draws out our heart to feel compassion and the love of God.

I am reminded of the Amish school children who were killed in 2006 by a local deliveryman. After he killed many of the children at the school, he killed himself leaving a wife and children. The Amish community, even in the midst of tremendous personal grief, rallied around the young mother and children expressing their forgiveness and support for them during their grief and affliction. The heart floods with emotion at the Christ-like compassion of these people. The whole world has been touched for good by their example.

When I was a young teenager, I was asked to stay overnight at a hospital in Charleston, SC, with a 16 year-old boy who had been involved in a terrible automobile accident. He had lost his right arm and was paralyzed from the neck down. Through the night, I had to turn him over every half hour, and often he would ask me to scratch his nose. He could not do anything for himself. When the morning came, I left the hospital filled with sadness for this young man but with gratitude for my countless blessings. I was so grateful to have the ability to care for myself and enjoy the freedom to move about and experience life with all of my senses. Observing his condition helped me to see my life through very different eyes.

Suffering also allows each of us the choice to turn toward God or away from God. **"But behold, because of the exceedingly great length of the war between the Nephites and the Lamanites many had become hardened, because of the exceedingly great length of the war; and many were softened because of their afflictions, insomuch that they did humble themselves before God, even in the depths of humility" (Alma 62:41).** Even though these people were all subjected to the same devastating conditions of war, some chose to become hardened and others became humble and submissive.

If our lives were soft and easy, God would never be considered. We would never turn to him in prayer or gratitude. We would place our trust in our own abilities and the arm of flesh. The apostle Paul relates, **"We must through much tribulation enter into the kingdom of God" (Acts 14:22).** Suffering allows for, and permits, the ultimate test of the human soul, the ultimate demonstration of faith. It is the opportunity to blame him or trust him and keep moving forward. Suffering must be viewed as the opportunity that God gives each of us to become like him. The purging is only finished upon the completion of mortality.

President John Taylor remarked that he heard the Prophet Joseph say in speaking to the Twelve on one occasion: "You have all kinds of trials to pass through, and it is quite as necessary for you to be tried even as Abraham, and other men of God. God will feel after you, he will take hold of you and wrench your very heartstrings, and if you cannot stand it you will not be fit for an inheritance in the Kingdom of God."[8] Each of us will and must be tried in areas of our lives that will make us fit to enter the Kingdom of God.

God spoke these words to Joseph Smith when Joseph felt that his personal suffering was too difficult to endure. **"Know thou, my son, that all these things shall give thee experience, and shall be for thy good. The Son of Man hath descended below them all. Art thou greater than he?" (D&C 122:7-8).** Christ set the example to help us see the value of our suffering and to help us realize that even he needed to suffer to gain all insight, understanding, and compassion.

We can see in the scriptures some of the alternative choices one faces while enduring adversity. Consider the attitudes of Christ and the two thieves while hanging on the cross. This account allows us to observe three levels of attitude while under extreme stress and pain, each a step closer to Godliness.

The first attitude expressed by one of the thieves is one of defiance, bitterness, and mockery. **"And one of the malefactors which were hanged railed on him, saying, if thou be Christ, save thyself and us" (Matthew 23:39).** This man was still blaming others for

79

the consequences of his choices. His heart was completely hardened.

The second attitude is one of contrition and an awareness of one's weakness and failings. **"But the other answering rebuked him, saying, dost not thou fear God, seeing thou art in the same condemnation? And we indeed justly; for we receive the due reward of our deeds: but this man hath done nothing amiss. And he said unto Jesus, Lord, remember me when thou comest into thy kingdom" (Matthew 23:40-42).** This malefactor had come to an awareness of his sins and his heart was open to call upon God.

The Savior demonstrates a third attitude as he teaches us the greater law. **"Then said Jesus, Father, forgive them; for they know not what they do" (Luke 23:34).** Christ took all of the previous attitudes to the highest level of love by forgiving those that hurt him just as the Amish people did in our previous account. They exhibited the ultimate in attitude: God-like charity.

We should rejoice in our affliction because we now have the opportunity, and are in a position, to demonstrate to God that we have faith in him under any circumstance. We can only exhibit this kind of faith here in mortality. There is no other time in our existence when we will have this opportunity, and there is no other way outside of suffering and trials to demonstrate our faith and develop our understanding of the Atonement.

God will bless us according to our attitude and faithfulness during affliction. **"He that is faithful in tribulation, the reward of the same is greater in the kingdom of heaven. Ye cannot behold with your** natural eyes, for the present time, the design of your God concerning those things which shall come hereafter, and the glory which shall follow after much tribulation. For after much tribulation come the blessings. Wherefore the day cometh that ye shall be crowned with much glory; the hour is not yet, but is nigh at hand" (D&C 58:2-4).** God also promises that, **"if thou endure it well, God shall exalt thee on high" (D&C 121:8).** His promised blessings are many if we approach our suffering with gratitude and humility.

Keep in mind that sometimes suffering is removed and sometimes the burden of suffering is lessened. We see this with the people of Alma. **"And now it came to pass that the burdens which were laid upon Alma and his brethren were made light; yea, the Lord did strengthen them that they could bear up their burdens with ease, and they did submit cheerfully and with patience to all the will of the Lord" (Mosiah 24:15).** Their burdens were made lighter through their faith and the blessings of God. They were also instructed in the purpose of their suffering when God said, **"...and this will I do that ye may stand as witnesses for me hereafter, and that ye may know of a surety that I, the Lord God, do visit my people in their afflictions" (Mosiah 24:14).** God wanted them to increase in their faith in him and to stand as witnesses of his great power to deliver each of us from bondage. Let it be understood that these people were a righteous people, and yet the Lord allowed them to suffer and to be brought into bondage.

It is necessary that there be resistance throughout our lives. **"For it must needs be, that there is an** opposition in all things" (2 Nephi 2:11). However, it is not necessary that we carry this suffering alone. "**Take my yoke upon you, and learn of me; for I am meek and lowly in heart: and ye shall find rest unto your souls**" **(Matt 11:39).** There is a reason why Christ is referred to as the Second Comforter. It is because he provides rest and comfort to our troubled souls.

Through our suffering we bring forth greater service to God's children. This is better explained in these verses: **"I am the true vine, and my Father is the husbandman. Every branch in me that beareth not fruit he taketh away: and every branch that beareth fruit, he purgeth it, that it may bring forth more fruit"** **(John 15:1-2).** We are constantly being purged so that we may be more useful to God and his children. Suffering is the only way we can become like God and are of the greatest benefit to our fellowman.

Job understood this as well as anyone when he said, **"when He hath tried me, I shall come forth as gold" (Job 23:10).** This was the comment of a man who had just lost all his material possessions, all of his children, and his health. He was almost completely alone, covered with boils, and suffering great physical and emotional privation and pain while still maintaining an attitude of respect, understanding, and gratitude toward God. He reflects this humble attitude upon learning of his great misfortunes when he states, **"Naked came I out of my mother's womb, and naked shall I return thither: the Lord gave, and the Lord hath taken away; blessed be the name of the Lord" (Job 1:21).** His wife even encouraged him to turn away from God. As Job sat among the ashes covered from head to toe with boils and in great physical and emotional pain she said, **"Dost thou still retain thine integrity? Curse God, and die" (Job 2:9).** Job responded with clear devotion to God by saying: **"What? shall we receive good at the hand of God, and shall we not receive evil?" (Job 2:10)** Through Job, we come to understand the higher law, one that teaches us to recognize God's blessings in all circumstances.

The heart swells with emotion as the Apostle John relates the blessed state of those who have suffered great affliction. **"After this I beheld, and, lo, a great multitude, which no man could number, of all nations, and kindreds, and people, and tongues, stood before the throne, and before the Lamb, clothed with white robes, and palms in their hands; … What are these which are arrayed in white robes? and whence came they? …And he said to me, These are they which came out of great tribulation, and have washed their robes, and made them white in the blood of the Lamb. Therefore are they before the throne of God, and serve him day and night in his temple: and he that sitteth on the throne shall dwell among them. They shall hunger no more, neither thirst any more; neither shall the sun light on them, nor any heat. For the Lamb which is in the midst of the throne shall feed them, and shall lead them unto living fountains of waters: and God shall wipe away all tears from their eyes" (Revelations 7:9, 13-17**). As I read this account, tears coursed down my face as my thoughts turned to the countless saintly people I have known over the years whose suffering was so great and often prolonged. It seemed so unfair and unjust. I realized that during their suffering they had made a choice, by their attitude and faith, to avoid murmuring. They chose to continue to seek the mercy of the Savior so that they might be washed in the blood of the Lamb.

# CREATION

This chapter discusses a very powerful healing concept. My personal healing began with the principle of faith, although I did not recognize what it was at the time. Faith is exercising our thoughts and words to bring about creation, the creation of a different way of thinking, loving, worshiping, and living. Faith in the Lord Jesus Christ is the basis of all change and healing.

In "Lectures on Faith," Joseph Smith states; "We ask, then, what are we to understand by a man's working by faith? We answer—we understand that when a man works by faith he works by mental exertion instead of physical force." Joseph Smith continues in saying, "It is by words, instead of exerting his physical powers, with which every being works when he works by faith. God said, 'Let there be light: and there was light'. Joshua spake, and the great lights which God had created stood still. Elijah commanded, and the heavens were stayed for the space of three years and six months, so that it did not rain: he again commanded and the heavens gave forth rain."[9]

All creation, both spiritual and physical, takes place through thoughts and words. **"For as he thinketh in his heart, so is he" (Proverbs 23:7).** William James describes the power of thought in this poem prefacing his best selling book, "As a Man Thinketh."

> Mind is the master power that molds and makes,
> And man is mind and ever more he takes,
> The tool of thought and shaping as he wills,
> Brings forth a thousand joys a thousand ills.
> He thinks in secret and it comes to pass.
> Environment is but his looking glass. [10]

It is a recorded fact in the scriptures that all things were created spiritually before they were created physically. **"For by the power of my Spirit created I them, yea, all things both spiritual and temporal...First spiritual, secondly temporal" (D&C 29:31-32). "For I the Lord God, created all things, of which I have spoken, spiritually before they were naturally upon the face of the earth" (Moses 3:5).** This gives us the pattern for creating things in our own lives.

Consider the concept of visualization, imagination, or thought. It is a mental or spiritual creation and the precursor to physical creation and action. If we think about our own dreams we will tend to agree that the images in our mind very often elicit emotions to the same extent as the real experience. A good example occurs when you wake up from a nightmare. Sometimes it is so vivid that you turn on the lights or play music to calm down, even though the experience was imaginary. Similarly, if we close our eyes and imagine biting into a pickle or a lemon, just the thought alone of biting into that vinegary pickle or that tart lemon causes our mouth to pucker and salivate. We are mentally creating a physical response to a pickle or lemon that does not exist.

In his narrative, *Return from Tomorrow*, George Richie makes another striking observation about his near death experience. While on the other side of the veil he views his life in vivid detail. He can see and feel the motivation behind his actions. He states that "thoughts (were) as observable as actions."[11] In other words, his thoughts were just as real in his mind as if he had physically performed them.

Is it any wonder the Lord says, **"Ye have heard it was said by them of old time, Thou shalt not commit adultery: But I say unto you, that whosoever looketh on a woman to lust after her hath committed adultery already in his heart" (Matt 5: 27-28).** We see that our thoughts are also closely tied to our hearts. Each thought occurring in the heart is an act of creation. We literally become the sum of our thoughts and create many of the conditions in our lives, maybe more than we realize.

In light of these scriptures and Richie's observation, things that we visualize are linked to reality and are actually occurring or have occurred, at least on a spiritual level. The same feelings we have when we do something physical are also manifest when we visualize. Even though these are images that we are creating in our mind, they are more effective if we see them as real and believe them to be real. The more clearly and focused we visualize while feeling the emotion, the more likely creation will take place on a physical level. These imaginings or thoughts can be for good or evil. Every action originates with the thought first. **"For out of the heart proceed evil thoughts, murders, adulteries, fornications, thefts, false witness, blasphemies" (Matthew 15:19).** People do not steal or kill without first thinking of stealing or killing.

It is the same with kind actions. One must think of, and ponder, kindness and compassion to become kind and compassionate. This is why it is so important to ponder the words of the Savior in the scriptures. By doing so, we may eventually become like the Savior. We will become what we choose to think and ponder.

There is a negative or a positive energy attached to each thought and word. The more intently we dwell on a thought and the more defined the detail, the more energy we give to it and the greater the likelihood of its physical creation. People who eventually fall into major sin have been focusing on it for some time. Just because we think about something does not mean it will materialize instantly. There must be a prolonged focus. We must also consider the intent behind our desires and if our desires are God's will for us.

At times, we may need to visualize something detrimental to be able to release a specific negative emotion. This may seem contrary to our current discussion on creating the positive. The intent and objective are key factors in any healing visualization. This will be clarified in more detail in Chapter 10, "Forgiveness and Judgment".

Many years ago, I was constantly asking God to give me an understanding of truth. I desired to find answers and know the truth. One night I found myself in an unusual dream. I was searching in a large city for someone that could teach me the truth I needed. I met a middle-aged woman and asked her if she could show me the truth. She asked me to follow her. We went into a large apartment building with many floors and took an elevator to one of the higher levels. There were many doors close together with an apartment behind each one. We walked the hallway until we came to a door that had a placard with one word on it. As I looked around, I noticed that all the other doors were blank. This door had the only placard on the entire floor. The word "IMAGINATION" was neatly printed on the placard.

I did not understand the meaning of this experience until some months later while reading a book by Betty J. Eadie. She made the following observation about her near death experience. "I understood that life is lived most fully in the imagination, that ironically, imagination is the key to reality. This is something I never would have supposed." [12]

The tower of Babel account in the Bible holds a little noticed concept. The people of Babel decided to build a tower to heaven, and the Lord came down to see the city and tower they were building. The Lord said, **"Behold, the people is one, and they have all one language; and this they begin to do: and now nothing will be restrained from them, which they have imagined to do" (Genesis 11: 4-6).** This may or may not have been a physical tower they were erecting. The important concept is that the people were one and unified as they imagined or visualized something the Lord did not want them to do. The Lord confounded their language to prevent their focused and unified efforts from being realized.

In contrast, the people of Enoch had their minds and hearts focused as one, but their focus was on God and his work. They were caught up into heaven and **"...the Lord called his people Zion, because they were of one heart and one mind" (Moses 7:18).** They placed their focus on righteousness and were blessed and obtained heaven. In a sense, they also built a tower to heaven, but the intent was completely different.

To facilitate our thoughts and creation, it is very helpful to ponder and visualize in a relaxed state or an alpha state. This is why God tells us to be still and to quiet the mind. The alpha state occurs when the brain is in a relaxed but focused and aware state. This is not sleep. We are very aware of everything taking place. In this state, the brainwaves run at about 8 to 12 cycles per second or hertz. Our normal awake state is the beta state when the brainwaves are at 13 to 25 hertz. After you practice relaxing and focusing your mental energy for a period of time, you can accomplish this relaxed state of mind instantaneously. In this relaxed condition, imagination is much more powerful and emotions can move out of the body more easily. Let us discover why this state of mind is so important.

The scriptures tell us that the Light of Christ is in and through all things. **"This is the light of Christ... And the light which shineth, which giveth you light, is** through him who enlighteneth your eyes, which is the same light that quickeneth your understandings; Which light proceedeth forth from the presence of God to fill the immensity of space— The light which is in all things, which giveth life to all things, which is the law by which all things are governed, even the power of God who sitteth upon his throne, who is in the bosom of eternity, who is in the midst of all things" (D&C 88:7, 11-13).** The Light of Christ is a universal energy, a web of energy that supports, sustains, and interconnects all things.

As we relax, our body and mind are more in tune with spiritual things, and we become more sensitive to this universal energy or Light of Christ. We also become more sensitive to the promptings of the Holy Ghost because our mind is still and quiet. This web of energy or Light of Christ contains all knowledge and truth because it emanates from Christ. It ties all of humanity together; it is our link as creations of God. This state of relaxation allows us to tune in to the Light of Christ, receive direction on what the Lord would have us do, receive help to remove the negative emotions, and change our hearts.

Joseph Smith also stated that words are a necessary part when one works by faith. Words, combined with the visual image of what we are seeking to create, increase the likelihood of its occurrence. The Savior warned of the power of our words when he said, **"But I say unto you, that every idle word that men shall speak, they shall give account thereof in the day of judgment. For by thy words thou shalt be justified, and by thy words thou shalt be condemned" (Matthew**

**12:36-37).** King Benjamin also cautioned us, **"Watch yourselves, and your thoughts, and your words, and your deeds" (Mosiah 4:30).** We should be careful with the words we use in our conversations and in our thought processes.

We should always accompany visualization with affirmations. An affirmation is a strong, positive statement that something is already so. Affirmations must be stated as if they already exist and must be kept short and concise. To affirm means to "make firm." Affirmations are best spoken aloud. Keep in mind that there is energy, for good or bad, attached to the words we speak. If we desire to be more compassionate, we might imagine ourselves serving another person who is suffering and say to ourselves, "I am compassionate and feel love for all of God's children. I find great joy in serving them."

Consider the following scriptures in relation to the power of our words: **"But I the Lord God, spake, and there went up a mist from the earth and watered the whole face of the ground" (Moses 3:6).**

**"And all nations feared greatly, so powerful was the word of Enoch, and so great was the power of the language which God had given him" (Moses 7:13).**

**"For behold, by the power of his word man came upon the face of the earth, which earth was created by the power of his word. Wherefore, if God being able to speak and the world was, and to speak and man was created, O then, why not be able to command the earth, or the workmanship of his hands upon the face of it according to His will and pleasure" (Jacob 4:9).**

We may ask ourselves why we do not make the changes we desire when we control and direct our thoughts and words. Thoughts and words are only part of the equation. Napoleon Hill said, "Whatever the mind of man can conceive and believe it can achieve."[13] It is vital that we believe the creative imaginations of our hearts. As we believe, we begin to feel the reality of our thoughts and creations taking place.

To demonstrate the power of belief, Bruce H. Lipton, refers to a study that was performed by Dr. Bruce Moseley in 2002 at the Baylor School of Medicine. In this study there were three groups of patients. Each group received surgery for their arthritic knees. Group one had damaged cartilage shaved in the knee. Group two had the knee flushed of material thought to cause the inflammation. The third group received only the standard surgical incision. Dr Moseley splashed water to simulate the sound of flushing the area. After 40 minutes the third group of patients were sewn up making them believe that they had received the standard accepted treatment, just like the first two groups. All three groups received the same aftercare, which included an exercise program.

The results of this study were profound. The first two groups improved as expected while the placebo group improved just as much as the other two. Dr. Moseley stated, "My skill as a surgeon had no benefit on these patients." [14] The strong belief of these patients brought about the miracles they experienced. Is this not the very concept the Savior tried to teach while here on earth? **"Go thy way; and as thou hast believed, *so* be it done unto thee" (Matthew 8:13). "Therefore I say unto you, what** things soever ye desire, when ye pray, believe that ye receive them, and ye shall have them" (Mark 11:24). "Be not afraid, only believe" (Mark 5:36). "If thou canst believe, all things are possible to him that believeth" (Mark 9:23).

The process of creation requires mental exertion, words, and belief. These criteria, along with understanding and following the will of God, allow us to accomplish his work and bring healing into our lives and the lives of others. It provides a way to deal with and overcome negative emotions, false beliefs, and irrational behaviors.

# FORGIVENESS AND JUDGMENT

Forgiveness is letting go of negative emotions such as hate, fear, resentment, guilt, and shame. It can be aided through the process of visualization or creation. True healing comes when we can finally replace these negative emotions with compassion and love.

As we pray, visualize, and verbalize our experiences, we have the opportunity to see differently and to change our perception. As long as we continue to see events and experiences in the same way our hearts cannot change. A key to healing emotionally and spiritually is to discover truth that will clear our misperceptions and negative feelings from our lives. With the help of the Savior, we can shift our negative feelings to feelings of compassion and love. We are seeking and asking for a personal truth that will cause a shift within our soul. Because visualization and thoughts have such an effect upon emotions, they are powerful tools to invite the Savior to help us create the compassion and understanding in the heart necessary to allow a complete letting go.

For instance, we may visualize an image of a person who has offended us approaching the Savior. As we imagine the interaction of the Savior with this person, we may come to realize that the Savior loves and cares about that person just as much as he loves us. He died for them too, not just for us. He is willing to heal them as well as us. The Atonement is for everyone. We may realize through the spirit that this person may have been abused as a child, come from a broken home or been through something that caused her to act out in a negative way. We may discover that we chose before we came to earth to go through certain difficult experiences, and we have been blaming God and been angry with him for many years for something we agreed to do. We may discover the blessings and gifts that we have because of the suffering and injustices we have endured.

When praying we should imagine being in the presence of the Savior and asking him questions directly. We should imagine his expressions and what he may say to us in response to our questions. It is critical that we ask the Savior to guide us to healing and forgiveness.

As we ask questions, let us keep in mind that the Holy Ghost is the revelator of the truths we seek. **"Yea, behold I will tell you in your mind and in your heart, by the Holy Ghost, which shall come upon you and which shall dwell in your heart. Now behold, this is the spirit of revelation" (D&C 8:2-3).** This spirit of revelation is the same spirit of revelation that clears your conscience of guilt, shame, and bitterness by replacing it with compassion and love. Consider again the experience of Enos in the Book of Mormon. **"And there came a voice unto me, saying: Enos, thy sins are forgiven thee, and thou shalt be blessed. And I, Enos, knew that God could not lie; wherefore, my guilt was swept away"** **(Enos 1:5-6).** The Lord spoke to his mind and heart through the Holy Ghost and cleared his conscience. The process of turning over and releasing negative emotions is a spiritual process, and it requires the spirit of the Lord.

The following example is unusual, but I use it because it demonstrates the power of our imagination. As we will see, we do not always know where our visualization may take us, but there are many places we can go in our mind's eye that we cannot and would not go in person.

I had an experience with a woman who harbored a terrible hatred toward a prior spouse for over 25 years. She had tried to run over her husband with a tractor when she discovered that he was involved with another woman. She had undergone three heart surgeries since her divorce. Her life was completely controlled by the anger she felt. As she brought her husband into her thoughts, she could feel nothing but contempt and the desire to destroy him. She wanted to hurt him in some way. She visualized herself beating and hurting him for several minutes and finally tired of the abuse she was inflicting upon him. After a while she turned to me and said, "I'm done; I don't want to do that anymore. I actually feel sorry

97

for him. I feel sorry for him because I can see his fear and sadness as a result of his prior unfaithfulness. I can see the effect it is having on him and the loss of respect and happiness in his life because of his actions." She allowed the Savior into her visualization and allowed the Savior to pick him up and begin to heal him. She allowed the light and love of the Savior to fill her and her prior husband and bring peace to her soul. She gained a perception that was founded in truth.

Visualizing the anger and destruction of another may seem contrary to what we learned about the power of creation in the preceding chapter. We certainly do not want to create something negative. In this example, we must consider the whole of the experience and not just the segments. Yes, she visualized harm to her prior husband, but subconsciously for many years she had been continually playing this hurtful film in her mind without resolution. She continued to hold to a false belief and allow the pain and anger to build in her heart. In this example, she was able to act out safely on a conscious level, destroy this belief, and release the negative emotions that she held in her heart for so many years. Visualization should only be performed with the intent to make the truth known on a conscious level so that we can lay down the incorrect belief, turn it over to the Savior, and remove it from the subconscious beliefs that we harbor to never be acted out again. This is much different than a person continually thinking of killing another and how that will be accomplished. Their visualization is prolonged and their intent is to kill, not to resolve emotional trauma.

This woman called me a week later and explained that she had been so physically sore from the visualization exercise that she had trouble getting out of bed for the three days following our visit. She also said that she felt only compassion and pity for her prior husband and was finally free of the debilitating anger and hate. She had to act out the hurt in her mind to gain a different perception and realize that his destruction was not what she wanted for him or her.

This may not be typical, but we are often surprised at how the spirit uses our subconscious to direct our feelings and to express images in our mind. Many times, our feelings are extremely intense.

Throughout our imaginings, we need to find a way to bring a "Christ perspective" to bear on the events so that we experience a change of heart. The scriptures tell us that the early disciples **"forgave not one another in their hearts" (D&C 64:8).** The Prophet Spencer W. Kimball stated that, "it must be a heart action and a purging of one's mind." [15]

Innocent victims, all of us at some time or another, may say, "I was a victim. It's not my fault that this person abused me. It's not fair that I'm required to forgive someone who continues to hurt others or is non-repentant. How can I forgive someone who ruined my life? I was young and couldn't protect myself, and I can't accept that the Lord expects me to forgive." No one is exempt from needing to forgive, even innocent victims. Forgiveness is as much, if not more for our benefit than it is for the offender. It allows us to free ourselves from the negative emotions associated with the experience.

There are no qualifications on whether we should forgive or not. If the person at fault feels no remorse and will not recognize what he has done, it does not make any difference, we are still required to forgive. **"But I say unto you, Love your enemies, bless them that curse you, do good to them that hate you, and pray for them which despitefully use you, and persecute you" (Matt. 5: 44).** This commandment is really for our well-being and healing. We encapsulate ourselves in pain and negative emotions until we release judgment and forgive.

I am impressed with the insights of author, Denver Snuffer, Jr. He makes some very powerful observations about accusing others. He relates the scriptural story of the woman who was taken in adultery and brought before the Savior. He states, "In spite of clear guilt, Christ found a way to avoid accusing her. This incident shows the length to which the Lord will go to avoid becoming the accuser. His title: "Our Advocate with the Father" is the antithesis of the role of the "accuser." The advocate helps defend us against accusations. Even accusations properly brought, as was the one against the woman taken in adultery. Certainly there are others who have offended you. Certainly you have just complaints about others. Christ is saying to forgive them anyway."

The author goes on to say that our judgment of others will set the standard by which we will be judged. He asks us to think of the condemnation we place upon ourselves at judgment time "in terms of having set a standard by judging others which you cannot meet when that standard is used against you. Help others face God without guilt of offenses they have caused you. Let them go free. Let the prison open and all who have ever caused you injury walk in the light of freedom free from any accusation you could bring against them. Forgive them for this because when they did so, they knew not what they did. Forgiving them will not just liberate them, but it will liberate you, as well. Letting go of the just accusation will not just let them out of their prison, but it will let you out of yours." [16] The scriptures refer to Satan as the **"accuser of our brethren…, which accused them before our God night and day" (Revelations 12:10).** We are following Satan's lead by accusing others of wrongdoing, even if we have a good reason to do so. It is our blessing when we forgive others, and it will open the floodgates of mercy.

Jesus illustrates the importance of forgiveness as he taught the disciples. **"Then came Peter to him, and said, Lord, how oft shall my brother sin against me, and I forgive him? till seven times? Jesus saith unto him, I say not unto thee, Until seven times: but, Until seventy times seven.**

**Therefore is the kingdom of heaven likened unto a certain king, which would take account of his servants. And when he had begun to reckon, one was brought unto him, which owed him ten thousand talents. But forasmuch as he had not to pay, his lord commanded him to be sold, and his wife, and children, and all that he had, and payment to be made. The servant therefore fell down, and worshipped him, saying, Lord, have patience with me, and I will pay thee all. Then the lord of that servant was moved with compassion, and loosed him, and forgave him the debt.**

But the same servant went out, and found one of his fellowservants, which owed him an hundred pence: and he laid hands on him, and took him by the throat, saying, Pay me that thou owest. And his fellowservant fell down at his feet, and besought him, saying, Have patience with me, and I will pay thee all. And he would not: but went and cast him into prison, till he should pay the debt. So when his fellow servants saw what was done, they were very sorry, and came and told unto their lord all that was done.

Then his lord, after that he had called him, said unto him, O thou wicked servant, I forgave thee all that debt, because thou desiredst me: Shouldest not thou also have had compassion on thy fellowservant, even as I had pity on thee? And his lord was wroth, and delivered him to the tormentors, till he should pay all that was due unto him. So likewise shall my Heavenly Father do also unto you, if ye from your hearts forgive not every one his brother their trespasses" (Matthew 18:21-35).** In this story the Lord tells us again to replace our anger and hurt with compassion and pity and to forgive from our hearts so that we can ensure our own forgiveness.

We go before God each day knowing that we are at his mercy for the sins we have committed. How can we expect his saving grace to be extended to us if we choose not to extend forgiveness to all others?

Judgment is the right of one individual, the Savior Jesus Christ. **"God shall judge the secrets of men by Jesus Christ according to my gospel" (Romans 2:16). "For the Father judgeth no man, but hath committed**

**all judgment unto the Son" (John 5:22).** I find great comfort in the fact that Christ will be our judge, knowing that he understands our pain, and he will advocate our case with pleadings before the throne of God, just as Enoch saw him do for the children of God who perished in the flood. **"And Christ "hath pled before my face. Wherefore, he suffereth for their sins" (Moses 7:39).**

We are the one person who will have an effect on the judgment that Christ will make. We determine the judgment that will be passed upon us by the Savior. **"Judge not, and ye shall not be judged: condemn not, and ye shall not be condemned: forgive, and ye shall be forgiven: Give, and it shall be given unto you; good measure, pressed down, and shaken together, and running over, shall men give into your bosom. For with the same measure that ye mete withal it shall be measured to you again" (Luke 6:37-38).** He will judge us based on our judgment of self and others.

When we are suffering from emotional trauma and sin, we become the most critical of judges. We often feel like no one understands our grief because we believe that others have not been through what we have been through or done what we have done. We are almost proud in our defiance of others' efforts to empathize. We look at others in relation to our own emotional problems and say to ourselves: "They have never been divorced. They were never sexually abused. They have never had major health problems. Their children are not wrapped up in drugs. Their parents were never divorced. Their dad was not an abusive alcoholic. They have never lost a loved one. Their mother did not leave them. How could they possibly

103

understand?" We spend so much time in self-pity and comparing ourselves to others that we feel a great amount of bitterness. We feel like no one really cares about us and yet we can be very unapproachable and filled with pride and indignity. We believe that others should be perfect when we ourselves are struggling.

On the other hand, we also judge ourselves very harshly as we make comparisons. We see others being successful, and we say to ourselves: "I will never amount to anything. I'm just a failure and I always will be. I'm stupid and can't learn anything. I don't have a chance because of my circumstances." We continue to be a victim and see everything from a victim's perspective.

To heal we must let ALL judgments go. We must stop comparing and suspend all judgment, realizing that we know absolutely nothing about the soul or trials of another. By judging, we intensify our negative emotions and block the spirit of the Lord.

We also learn something about our own faults and failings in the following verse. **"Therefore thou art inexcusable, O man, whosoever thou art that judgest: for wherein thou judgest another, thou condemnest thyself; for thou that judgest doest the same things. But we are sure that the judgment of God is according to truth against them which commit such things. And thinkest thou this, O man, that judgest them which do such things, and doest the same, that thou shalt escape the judgment of God?" (Romans 2:1-3).** This verse appears to be in reference to the verses in the prior chapter of Romans 1:26-32. Many sins are listed in those verses, and those who judge are surely committing at least one of these sins themselves.

We really have no right to judge because we also have sins. On the other hand, as we forgive, suspend judgment, return our focus to serving others, and realize that we are all the same in the eyes of God, we will be lifted up and shown great mercy and grace in spite of our imperfections.

# OUR TRUE NATURE

Our true nature gives us insight into what and who we really are in relation to God and what he intends for us. As we understand this relationship, our perception changes and allows greater healing. Men and women are continually changing and becoming. The majority of us drift with no end in sight. As with any goal, we only accomplish what we can conceive. The four-minute mile was considered impossible until Roger Banister ran it. Others soon began to break four minutes and today it is a common occurrence for many high school runners to do it. To heal emotionally, it is necessary to see the truth about our nature and understand our possibilities. This creates personal hope and faith in our ability to make changes. We learn that **"God created man in his own image" (Genesis 1:27)** and our future is designed to be one of glory and happiness. He promises that if we meet certain conditions **"all that [our] Father hath shall be given unto [us]" (D&C 84:38).** He considers us so important that he wants us to have all that he has.

We are God's children, and we bring him glory as we become like him. Our righteousness magnifies and increases his glory. God tells us specifically, **"This is my work and my glory—to bring to pass the immortality and eternal life of man" (Moses 1:39).** If his glory is magnified by our success, it follows that his greatest desire is for us to become like him and become successful and happy. Just as parents experience pride in the successes of their children, God experiences great joy as we follow his example.

God takes no pleasure in our poor choices and failures but in our success, happiness, and joy. God wants us to understand his depth of feeling when he says, **"Have I any pleasure at all that the wicked should die? …. and not that he should return from his ways, and live? For I have no pleasure in the death of him that dieth….wherefore turn yourselves, and live ye" (Ezekiel 18:23,32).** He is pleading with us to turn to him and live. It saddens him for us to do otherwise. He sees our pain and wants us to have the joy he experiences as a perfect being. He tells us that **"men are, that they might have joy" (2 Nephi 2:25**). God created a plan for us with the express purpose in mind that we might have joy. God seeks our happiness, which in turn brings about his glory.

For man to be completely happy, we must become exactly like him in character and aspect. President Lorenzo Snow said, "As man now is, God once was; as God now is, man may be." [17] This idea and truth was not original to President Snow. The Prophet Joseph Smith preached the following concept in 1844. "God himself was once as we are now, and is an exalted man, and sits enthroned in yonder heavens! That is the great secret. If the veil were rent today, and the great God who holds this world in its orbit, and who upholds all worlds and all things by His power, was to make himself visible, I say, if you were to see him today, you would see him like a man in form—like yourselves in all the person, image, and very form as a man; for Adam was created in the very fashion, image and likeness of God, and received instruction from, and walked, talked and conversed with Him, as one man talks and communes with another."[18] Does this mean we have the seeds of godhood, and we are designed to become gods and goddesses? Absolutely, this is what we are designed to be by our maker. We are his offspring. A cow has never given birth to a bird, and the radish seed does not become a head of lettuce. We are destined to be gods and goddesses and to be like him. It defies reason to think otherwise.

When God created us, we knew that we were his children with the potential to be like him. The Apostle Paul understood our relationship to God when he said; **"For we are also his offspring...we are the offspring of God" (Acts 17:18-19).** God also makes it clear when he tells Moses, **"Thou art my son.... thou art in the similitude of mine Only Begotten" (Moses 1:4,6,7).** During this conversation, God called Moses his son three separate times. Later in the same chapter, Satan appeared to Moses but did not want Moses to understand his potential. **"Satan came tempting him, saying: Moses, son of**

**man, worship me" (Moses 1:12).** Satan wanted Moses to think and feel that he was not a son of God but of man.

Jesus understood the nature of man and his potential to become like god. He quoted scripture that referred to each of us as gods or potential gods. **"Jesus answered them, Is it not written in your law, I said, Ye are gods? If he called them gods, unto whom the word of God came, and the scripture cannot be broken; Say ye of him, whom the Father hath sanctified, and sent into the world, Thou blasphemest; because I said, I am the Son of God" (John 10:33-36).** This scripture reminded the Jews that God had referred to the people as gods in prior scripture. Christ's reference to himself as the Son of God was in keeping with the word of God.

We are all at different levels of growth along this road to godhood, but each of us can arrive. **"Behold, he sendeth an invitation unto all men, for the arms of mercy are extended towards them" (Alma 5:33).** He offers this to all of his children because of his great love for them.

When is the last time you actually imagined yourself as one having godlike qualities? What is the image you carry around in your mind about yourself and your potential?

As stated earlier, man is in the image of God. Man is not an exact duplicate of him in appearance, but he is the same in form and composed of the same elements. Our bodies and our spirits consist of matter, or in other words, energy. "Einstein showed that mass and energy are equivalent: the property called mass is simply concentrated energy. In other words, matter is energy and energy is matter, and the distinction is simply one of a temporary state."[19]

Our bodies and our physical surroundings are only energy moving at a much slower frequency than our spirit. God revealed through Joseph Smith, **"There is no such thing as immaterial matter. All spirit is matter, but it is more fine or pure, and can only be discerned by purer eyes; we cannot see it; but when our bodies are purified we shall see that it is all matter" (D&C 131: 7-8).** Our bodies reside in the same location as our spirits because the spirit inside is a finer matter or energy.

We could also suppose that other kingdoms could reside in the same location as our earthly kingdom. The Lord revealed that **"all kingdoms have a law given; And there are many kingdoms; for there is no space in the which there is no kingdom; and there is no kingdom in which there is no space, either a greater or a lesser kingdom" (D&C 88:36-37).** This could explain the immense creations of God. Moses writes, **"and were it possible that man could number the particles of the earth, yea, millions of earths like this, it would not be a beginning to the number of thy creations" (Moses 7:30).** It is very possible that God's creations reside at many levels of finer matter or frequencies in some of the same locations. In this way space could provide an infinite amount of room for creation.

Spirits, being a finer matter and being purer, exist at a higher vibratory rate or energy frequency than our earthly body. **"Even ye shall receive your bodies, and your glory shall be that glory by which your bodies**

110

**are quickened" (D&C 88:28).** It is my personal belief that through the resurrecting power of Christ the spirit and body will be quickened to provide a permanent union and an eternal bond linking the spirit and elements as one. **"For man is spirit. The elements are eternal, and spirit and element, inseparably connected, receive a fullness of joy" (D&C 93:33).** The result or vibratory rate of this union will be determined by our purity and level of light and knowledge.

God is a being of light. **"God is light and in him is no darkness at all" (1 John 1:5).** Do not be confused that God is light and is also tangible. Joseph Smith taught, **"The Father has a body of flesh and bones as tangible as man's; the Son also" (D&C 130:22).** How can God be both light and tangible? Light is composed of photons filled with quantified amounts of energy and information. In other words, light is also considered energy, and energy is also matter as we just discussed. Therefore, because of God's level of perfection, he emits an enormous amount of light while also maintaining mass.

The Apostle John spoke of this tremendous glory and light in the Book of Revelations when he spoke of the Holy City. He said, **"And the city had no need of the sun, neither of the moon, to shine in it: for the glory of God did lighten it, and the Lamb is the light thereof" (Revelations 21:23).**

Light is also nature's way of transferring energy through space. Consider the account of Moroni's visit to Joseph Smith. **"While I was thus in the act of calling upon God, I discovered a light appearing in my room, which continued to increase until the room was** lighter than at noonday, when immediately a personage appeared at my bedside" (JS History 1:30). Joseph Smith also described the visit of God the Father and Christ in these words. **"I saw a pillar of light exactly over my head, above the brightness of the sun, which descended gradually until it fell upon me. ...When the light rested upon me I saw two Personages, whose brightness and glory defy all description, standing above me in the air" (JS History 1:16-17).** With each appearance there was light accompanying the being to the specific location.

His offspring, you and I, are also constructed of the same elements but not yet perfected. In the scriptures, God is referred to as the **"Father of Lights" (James 1:17, D&C 67:9).** God is light and God is our Father. He is the Father of lights. We are his children, and therefore we have light or knowledge within us. Light is also synonymous with knowledge and truth.

**"Man was also in the beginning with God. Intelligence, or the light of truth, was not created or made, neither indeed can be. All truth is independent in that sphere in which God has placed it, to act for itself, as all intelligence also; otherwise there is no existence. The glory of God is intelligence, or, in other words, light and truth" (D&C 93:29-30,36).** We previously mentioned that man's eternal life is God's work and glory, therefore we may very well be the intelligence or the light of truth referred to in this passage.

We were in the beginning with God, and we were all intelligences residing at different levels of progression. God took these intelligences and clothed them with spirits.

112

He allowed these spirits to come to earth to obtain a body. The Prophet Spencer W. Kimball outlines this process. "God has taken these intelligences and given to them spirit bodies and given them instructions and training. Then he proceeded to create a world for them and sent them as spirits to obtain a mortal body, for which he made preparation. And when they were upon the earth, he gave them instructions on how to go about developing and conducting their lives to make them perfect, so they could return to their Father in Heaven after their transitions."[20]

Based on this discussion, it only makes sense that between our intelligence, spirit, and body, we also consist of the light and truth. **"Ye were also in the beginning with the Father; that which is Spirit, even the Spirit of truth" (D&C 93:23).** Therefore, being in God's likeness, we have the capacity to become like God in every respect.

We thrive and grow in God's light; the light of Christ is in and through all the creations of God. **"Which light proceedeth forth from the presence of God to fill the immensity of space— The light which is in all things, which giveth life to all things, which is the law by which all things are governed, even the power of God who sitteth upon his throne, who is in the bosom of eternity, who is in the midst of all things" (D&C 88:12-13).** The light of Christ maintains life and all the creations of God.

When we go against the laws of God, we allow darkness to displace the light of Christ. Even though we are also beings of light, our light is insufficient to sustain our progress and growth in this mortal setting without the light of Christ. In fact, our personal light can be nearly extinguished through unrighteous living or as a result of serious trauma. We are in a growth and maturation process and the light of Christ is necessary to support, strengthen, and guide our growth until the perfect day. We are spiritual beings that receive our sustaining and supporting light from God.

God tells us to **"search diligently in the light of Christ that ye may know good from evil" (Moroni 7:19).** It is in this light that we gain understanding. This light also helps us to remember the knowledge we received when we were in the pre-existence with God.

What can the light of Christ do for our bodies and spirits other than provide knowledge and understanding? Our bodies consist of atoms and each atom has a nucleus at its center and negatively charged electrons that orbit around the nucleus. In a simple atom, if the electron is undisturbed, it is generally bound tightly and exists in an inactive ground state until exposed to light. When light hits the atom a certain photon or number of photons carrying energy and information may have just the right frequency to interact with the electron in the atom. The photon is absorbed into the atom, and the electron is elevated into an excited state. Depending on how many of these photons are absorbed determines to what level the electrons are excited.

It is my supposition that, as the light of Christ intensifies and the Holy Ghost operates upon our bodies and spirits on a regular basis, our cells are elevated to higher levels of frequency by the absorption of this energy.

Something else occurs after the atom is excited. The excited atoms also expel the energy that was absorbed by the electron and the atom returns to a state of inactivity. If the atom is no longer exposed to the light source, it will remain inactive. I believe that light is a result of the constant expulsion of energy from within. If we remain open to the light of Christ and the Holy Ghost through our obedience, gratitude, and positive focus, our atoms will continue in an excited state on a regular basis. In other words, we will be in a state of sanctification and spiritual growth until the perfect day.

To become like God, we must seek to be filled with his light. We are instructed to **"cast off the works of darkness, and let us put on the armour of light" (Romans 13:12).** When we suffer from sin or abuse, we are usually enveloped in darkness. Allowing the light of the Savior into our soul is an important key to our healing. His light restores and magnifies our light until the perfect day. **"I am come a light into the world, that whosoever believeth on me should not abide in darkness" (John 12:46)** We allow the light of Christ to affect our lives through the concepts previously discussed such as willingness, humility, gratitude, and a focus on Christ.

The scriptures also speak about the cleansing influence of the light that emanates from the Savior when he appeared to the people of the American continent after his resurrection. **"And it came to pass that Jesus blessed them as they did pray unto him; and his countenance did smile upon them, and the light of his countenance did shine upon them, and behold they were as white as the countenance and also the**

115

garments of Jesus; and behold the whiteness thereof did exceed all the whiteness, yea, even there could be nothing upon earth so white as the whiteness thereof. And he turned from them again, and went a little way off and bowed himself to the earth; and he prayed again unto the Father, saying: Father, I thank thee that thou hast purified those whom I have chosen, because of their faith" (3 Nephi 19:25, 27-28).** There appears to be a relationship between the light he exposed them to and the purification process.

We can visualize and imagine the Savior and his light emanating from him and entering our heart and soul, cleansing and healing our hearts. We can imagine his light moving through our past experiences, and removing and cleansing our negative feelings. We can imagine ourselves with the Savior in any way we desire so that we might feel his healing power and influence.

We are children of a God, and his blessings are available to each of us. We are his most important creation. We can become like him in every way. Our ultimate destiny is godhood and our greatest benefactor will be God the Father.

# IMAGINING THE IDEAL

Imagining our ideal self is necessary to healing. The reason we do this is so that we know where we are trying to go and what we are trying to become. When we start out on any trip, we always have a destination in mind. It is absurd to think of taking a trip without knowing where we are going. Everything we accomplish in our lives must be viewed mentally prior to its accomplishment. There are three eyes with which we see, the two physical eyes and the eye of the mind or the eye of faith. Eastern philosophers refer to this as the third eye or spiritual eye.

The scriptures tell us, **"And if your eye be single to my glory your whole bodies shall be filled with light, and there shall be no darkness in you; and that body which is filled with light comprehendeth all things. Therefore, sanctify yourselves that your minds become single to God, and the days will come that you shall see him" (D&C 88:67-68).** Our spiritual eye is the one referred to in this scripture. It is interchangeable with our mind or our mental vision.

As with any goal, imagining our ideal self must be defined and determined in the greatest detail possible. The more detailed, the more likely we will succeed in the process. As we consider ourselves based on our true nature, as we previously discussed, what is the image we want to project of ourselves? We must think about the attributes of the Savior such as strength, compassion, confidence, love, courage, and other positive characteristics. Once we can see ourselves with all of the qualities and appearance we desire, we need to use all of our senses as we imagine it. Hear our voice, see color, touch, smell, and feel what it is like to be this person. We must see ourselves in action. The more we use the senses in our image, the greater creative strength will be manifest. We must imagine what it would feel like to be the person we see in our mind's eye. We must imagine that we are already this way. If we can do this, we may be certain that changes are possible.

If we cannot see ourselves, and the desired characteristics, we should try to bring the Savior and his light and compassion into our imagination to assist in this process. When I tried to see myself in my mind many years ago, I could only see a black object. My self worth was at an all-time low. I imagined that I was in a black bag and saw the Savior opening the bag and allowing the bag to fall away. I imagined his light filling me and healing me as I came out from the darkness. It was a very powerful experience. You may see it another way, but the Lord will help you see it in a way that will allow healing.

We need to know that we can create anything we desire in our minds. We are the only limiting factor to becoming what God would have us be. As we see the Savior in our mind, we should ask him questions and watch and listen to him respond to those questions. I often use this method when I pray, asking God questions and listening for answers.

Once we can see ourselves, we can entertain the thought that we really are this image. It also helps to describe our ideal self by expressing our attributes out-loud. We discussed affirmations in Chapter 9 and how this allows another part of the creative process to work and creation to magnify its work.

The prophets taught this very important principle of seeing things as if they already existed. **"Wherefore, the prophets, and the priests, and the teachers, did labor diligently, persuading them to look forward unto the Messiah, and believe in him to come, as though he already was" (Jarom 1:11).** King Benjamin also tells his people to **"rejoice with exceedingly great joy, even as though [Christ] had already come among them" (Mosiah 3:13).** The people were taught to look forward with faith in Christ and act and imagine as if he had already come. Being able to see something as if it has already happened pushes faith to a new level and brings forth the fruits of our faith.

We must see our outcome and believe as if it already exists. We should see ourselves as patient, kind, and helpful. We must see ourselves serving others in need. If we hold the priesthood, we should see ourselves blessing and healing the sick and preaching the Gospel with power and by the spirit. We must imagine sharing our testimony with others. We must see ourselves kneeling across the holy alter from a worthy spouse in the temple and receiving the sealing ordinances. We should imagine ourselves in a positive and loving relationship with our spouse and children. We must see ourselves teaching our children and making a difference. We should see ourselves being faithful to God in all things, and eventually greeting the Savior and hearing the words, "Well done my good and faithful servant, enter into the rest of the Lord."

We should imagine being reunited with family and loved ones in the after life and receiving all the blessings that God has in store for us. We must experience all the sights, sounds, smells, and physical feelings as we go through this exercise. **"Jesus said unto him, If thou canst believe, all things *are* possible to him that believeth" (Mark 9:23).** We cannot become something we cannot or will not imagine or see in our mind's eye. We are limited in our progress only by our beliefs and imagination.

# QUIET THE MIND

It is very important that we learn to live in the present by quieting our minds. The ability to focus our thoughts will promote our healing as well as keep us from creating and harboring additional negative emotions. It also opens our minds to the voice of the Lord. We must be very protective and control our thoughts. We must not dwell on past mistakes or what should have been. By staying in the present we will experience a much fuller and enjoyable life. **"Let not your minds turn back" (D&C 67:14).** We can act only in the present to affect the present and the future.

Some of us feel it is too late in our lives to make changes and accomplish God's work. We may believe we have missed our opportunities. God can do all things and he can accomplish great things through a child as well as an aged person. Consider the prophet Mormon who led the Nephite armies at the young age of sixteen. Consider Abraham's wife, Sarah, who gave birth to Isaac when she was ninety years of age. All things are possible with God.

It is also important that we not dwell on the future. This does not mean we should forego planning the future. It means we should focus on what we can do today to prepare for it and place our faith in God that his will may be accomplished. The future will never play out exactly as we plan because our plan is not generally the Lord's plan. It is also not healthy or productive to think we must wait twenty years to accomplish things when we are retired, the house is paid off or the kids are grown. We can accomplish great and important things right now.

If we will observe our thoughts, we will notice that very little of our time is spent focusing on the moment, the here and now. All healing takes place in the moment, not in the future. Building present awareness has been taught in many religions and philosophies. Let us take a few moments and focus on what we are hearing, seeing, smelling, tasting, and feeling right now. Let us pay attention to our breathing and our movements, to the sensation and feel of our clothes against our skin. Let us quiet the busy self-talk that takes us nowhere and can be very negative. The more we practice this exercise the more often we will find ourselves focused on the present. At first we will struggle, but it will become second nature if we continue. In this state of mind, the Lord can speak to our hearts and minds and display his majesty.

To illustrate the power of stillness, the following experience occurred as I was walking around an elementary school playground at five o'clock in the morning. I was trying to keep my focus in the present and pay attention to the moment and the early morning sounds, when all at once, I heard in my mind the sound of thousands of voices singing and conversing in happy chattering. I was surprised at the amount of noise that I perceived and I began to look around. As I searched around me, a strong impression came into my mind that I was hearing the intelligences in nature, in particular the millions of blades of grass on the school playground.

I realize this may seem odd but it was an indicator that I was gaining better control of my mind and coming closer to knowing God and his creations. All things have an intelligence and each has come to earth at a different level of progress and organization. Abraham learned from the Lord that there are different levels of intelligences. **"These two facts do exist, that there are two spirits, one being more intelligent than the other: there shall be another more intelligent than they; I am the Lord thy God, I am more intelligent than they all" (Abraham 3:18-21).**

The scriptures often attribute intelligent characteristics to nature. **"For ye shall go out with joy, and be led forth with peace: the mountains and the hills shall break forth before you into singing, and all the trees of the field shall clap their hands" (Isaiah 55:12).**

Enoch tells us that he, **"looked upon the earth; and he heard a voice from the bowels thereof, saying: Wo, wo is me, the mother of men; I am pained, I am weary, because of the wickedness of my children. When shall I rest and be cleansed from the filthiness which is gone forth out of me?...And when Enoch heard the earth mourn, he wept..." (Moses 7:48-49).** In this case the earth spoke out as an intelligence.

Christ also said, during his triumphal ride into Jerusalem, **"I tell you that, if these should hold their peace, the stones would immediately cry out" (Luke 19:40).** I personally believe that Christ was literal in his reference to the stones. They would have cried out.

God understands the importance of quieting the mind. The prophets have asked that we ponder. If we are to hear the voice of the Lord as we ponder, we need to stop the constant chatter of the mind.

An exercise I do to quiet my mind is to relax and imagine that I am throwing a stone into a pool of water. I watch the ripples move away from the stone. I watch the ripples go out into the universe and observe and feel the peace of nature and space. Allow yourself to experience God's quiet creations.

Consider these scriptures as you work to quiet your mind and become more in tune with yourself, God's creations, and the Spirit.

"Hearken unto this, O Job: **stand still**, and consider the wondrous works of God" (Job 37:14).

"Therefore, let your hearts be comforted concerning Zion; for all flesh is in mine hands; **be still** and know that I am God" (D&C 101:16).

"Therefore, dearly beloved brethren, let us cheerfully do all things that lie in our power; and then **may we stand still**, with the utmost assurance, to see the salvation of God, and for his arm to be revealed" (D&C 123:17).

"Whereas **ye know not what *shall be* on the morrow**. For what *is* your life? It is even a vapour, that appeareth for a little time, and then vanisheth away" (James 4:14).

"**In your patience** possess ye your souls" (Luke 21:19).

"Therefore, **take ye no thought for the morrow**, for what ye shall eat, or what ye shall drink, or wherewithal ye shall be clothed. For, consider the lilies of the field, how they grow, they toil not, neither do they spin; and the kingdoms of the world, in all their glory, are not arrayed like one of these. For your Father, who is in heaven, knoweth that you have need of all these things. Therefore, let the morrow take thought for the things of itself. **Neither take ye thought beforehand** what ye shall say; but treasure up in your minds continually the words of life, and it shall be given you in the very hour that portion that shall be meted unto every man" (D&C 84:81-85).

# GRATITUDE

Gratitude provides an additional key to emotional healing. It lifts our spirit and brings power into our lives. Let us consider how we feel when someone expresses gratitude to us. The words sink deep into our hearts and we feel the spirit. We are glad we helped them and will be glad to help again. God responds in a similar manner. **"And he who receiveth all things with thankfulness shall be made glorious; and the things of this earth shall be added unto him, even an hundred fold, yea, more" (D&C 78:19).** As we praise and thank him, I believe it invites and allows him to bless us by giving us strength and providing miracles in our lives.

Merlin Carothers, a Christian Minister, relates a vision he experienced while attending a camp retreat. He saw a beautiful, bright summer's day and noticed up above a heavy, solid black cloud beyond which nothing could be seen. A ladder extended from the ground through the cloud and beyond. There was a crowd of people at the bottom trying to climb the ladder. They had heard there was something wonderful on the other side of the cloud. As people would reach the cloud and begin to enter, they would lose their balance and fall into the crowd and scatter and hurt the people. They reported that they lost their direction upon entering the cloud.

When Merlin climbed the ladder into the cloud, he said that the darkness was so intense he was nearly forced to retreat back down the ladder. Step-by-step he continued until he came out the other side where he saw "a brilliant whiteness too glorious to describe in words. As I came out above the dark cloud I realized I could walk on top of it. As I looked into the brightness I was able to walk without difficulty… Only by looking at the brightness could I stay on top."

He recounted that the scene changed, and he could see three levels. He asked God what it all meant. In his words he recounts, "The brightest sunshine below the cloud is the light that many Christians live in and accept as normal. The ladder is the ladder of praising Me. Many try to climb and learn to praise Me in all things. At first they are very eager, but when they get into things that they don't understand they become confused and cannot hold on. They lose faith and go sliding back."

"Those who make it through those difficult times reach a new world and realize that the life they once thought of as normal cannot be compared to the life I have prepared for those who praise Me and believe that I carefully watch over them. He who reaches the light of the Heavenly kingdom can walk on top of difficulties no matter how dark they may seem as long as he keeps his eyes off the problem and on … Christ."[21]

Should we thank God for our trials as well as our blessings? **"Rejoice ever more. Pray without ceasing. In every thing give thanks: for this is the will of God in Christ Jesus concerning you" (1 Thessalonians 5:16-18).** We should thank God for all things.

What is included in all things? If we are sick-let us give thanks, if we have lost a loved one- let us give thanks, if we lost our job- let us give thanks, if we have a child who is struggling- let us give thanks, if we are in prison- let us give thanks, if our car breaks down- let us give thanks, if we have been abused- let us give thanks, if we are still being abused- let us give thanks, if we are struggling with marital problems- let us give thanks… no matter what the trial we should give thanks. When we truly look at our lives, the greatest amount of growth takes place in the fire of affliction. This is when we are purified.

The Apostle Paul understood this concept. **"And he said unto me, My grace is sufficient for thee: for my strength is made perfect in weakness. Most gladly therefore will I rather glory in my infirmities, that the power of Christ may rest upon me. Therefore I take pleasure in infirmities, in reproaches, in necessities, in persecutions, in distresses for Christ's sake: for when I am weak, then am I strong" (2 Corinthians 12:9-10).** The trials we suffer can make us strong and humble or weak and fearful. We may start out weak and afraid, but we can choose the course of our responses as we deal with the trial. It is very important that we endure suffering and trials with praise and gratitude.

If we believe our pain and anger are so great that it is difficult to find the ability to express gratitude and praise, it may help to write out a list beginning with certain physical attributes such as eyes, ears, fingers, and so on. Let us look for the little things that make a huge difference in our quality of life. Speaking gratitude for them aloud may allow us to see a new perspective and humble ourselves and make it easier to feel the need to offer thanks to God for those things that appear to be a difficulty in our lives.

We learn in the scriptures that thanksgiving is a powerful key to unlock communication with the Lord. It is so important that it is mentioned with prayer in the scriptures many times. It is interesting that many scriptures on prayer speak only of offering thanksgiving. The prophet Daniel **"kneeled upon his knees three times a day, and prayed, and gave thanks before his God" (Daniel 6:10).** In relation to the temple duties of the Levites the scriptures state that they were **"to stand every morning to thank and praise the Lord, and likewise at even" (1 Chronicles 23:30).** In this scripture we see that there are two parts to gratitude. We are to thank God, and we are to praise God.

When the Jaredites were in the throws of the sea coming to the American continent, **"They did sing praises unto the Lord; yea, the brother of Jared did sing praises unto the Lord, and he did thank and praise the Lord all the day long; and when the night came, they did not cease to praise the Lord" (Ether 6:9).** When Jesus healed the ten lepers, **"One of them, when he saw that he was healed, turned back, and**

129

with a loud voice glorified God, (praised) And fell down on his face at his feet, giving him thanks: and he was a Samaritan" (Luke 17: 15-16).

Most of us know how to give thanks and these scriptures teach that we should thank him for all of our experiences, good and bad. Offering praise, however may be something many of us have never experienced. As we study the Prophets, we find many examples of prayers being offered up in praise unto God. The prophet Lehi gives a short example of what one might say in praising God.

"And it came to pass that when my father had read and seen many great and marvelous things, he did exclaim many things unto the Lord; such as: Great and marvelous are thy works, O Lord God Almighty! Thy throne is high in the heavens, and thy power, and goodness, and mercy are over all the inhabitants of the earth; and, because thou art merciful, thou wilt not suffer those who come unto thee that they shall perish! And after this manner was the language of my father in the praising of his God; for his soul did rejoice, and his whole heart was filled, because of the things which he had seen, yea, which the Lord had shown unto him" (1 Nephi 1:14-15). The scriptures teach us that thanking and praising are different. We thank God for our specific blessings and trials, and we praise God in his grand and glorious majesty.

It is not surprising that the principle of gratitude provides great healing blessings once we realize how God feels when we do not give him the credit for his tender mercies. **"And in nothing doth man offend God, or against none is his wrath kindled, save those who confess not his hand in all things, and obey not his commandments" (D&C 59:21).** After all, God has given us everything, even our very lives.

The Prophet Nathan was sent by the Lord to revile and curse King David for killing Uriah and taking Uriah's wife Bathsheba for his own. Nathan said, **"Thus saith the Lord God of Israel, I anointed thee king over Israel, and I delivered thee out of the hand of Saul; And I gave thee thy master's house, and thy master's wives into thy bosom, and gave thee the house of Israel and of Judah; and if that had been too little, I would moreover have given unto thee such and such things. Wherefore hast thou despised the commandment of the Lord, to do evil in his sight? thou hast killed Uriah the Hittite with the sword, and hast taken his wife to be thy wife, and hast slain him with the sword of the children of Ammon" (2 Samuel 12:7-9).** David had everything; the Lord had lifted him in every circumstance, and yet he was still not satisfied. Let us learn from David's great error.

Even though we have difficulties, trials, and even abuses, we must remember that God will bless us if we look for and acknowledge his mercies.

D&C 98:1 ...**and in everything give thanks;**

D&C 46:7 But ye are commanded in all things to ask of God, who giveth liberally; and that which the Spirit testifies unto you even so I would that ye should do in all holiness of heart, walking uprightly before me, considering the end of your salvation, **doing all things with prayer and thanksgiving**, that ye may not be seduced by evil spirits, or doctrines of devils, or the commandments of men; for some are of men, and others of devils.

D&C 136:28 ...praise the Lord with singing, with music, with dancing, and with **a prayer of praise and thanksgiving**.

D&C 59:7 Thou shalt **thank the Lord thy God in all things**.

Alma 37:37 and when thou risest in the morning **let thy heart be full of thanks unto God**; and if ye do these things, ye shall be lifted up at the last day.

Alma 7:23 ...**always returning thanks unto God** for whatsoever things ye do receive.

Alma 34:38 ...and that ye **live in thanksgiving daily**, for the many mercies and blessings which he doth bestow upon you.

Ephesians 5:20 **Giving thanks always** for all things unto God and the Father in the name of our Lord Jesus Christ;

Colossians 3:17 ... do all in the name of the Lord Jesus, **giving thanks to God** and the Father by him.

Mosiah 2: 20-21 ...if **you should render all the thanks and praise which your whole soul has power to possess**, to that God who has created you, and has kept and preserved you...21... yet ye would be unprofitable servants.

Mosiah 24:21 Yea, and in the valley of Alma **they poured out their thanks to God** because he had been merciful unto them, and eased their burdens, and had delivered them out of bondage...

Mosiah 26:39 ...being commanded of God to pray without ceasing, and to **give thanks in all things**.

# SERVICE

$A$s we serve God's children, his spirit will work its healing influence upon our emotions and souls. The key is to focus outward for **"whosoever will save his life shall lose it; but whosoever shall lose his life for my sake and the gospel's, the same shall save it" (Mark 8:35).**

The work and glory of God is to save his children. We assist him by bringing comfort and light into their lives. **"Inasmuch as ye have done it unto one of the least of these my brethren, ye have done it unto me" (Matthew 25:40).**

After many months of struggling with depression and being unable to work, a close friend asked me if I would work in a new treatment center for juvenile delinquents. I had attempted several jobs with little to no success, and I was terrified by the idea. As I began working and could see my efforts were helping others, I could literally feel the healing impact it was having on me. I realized that my pain was not the only pain in the world, and it was also not the greatest pain. Others struggled as much and many times more than I did. The new perspective I gained from serving these youth began to work upon my feelings and added healing to my soul. I suppose this is why many people who have suffered through abuses and difficult circumstances try to go into psychology and counseling.

We do not need to work with juvenile delinquents to find healing. There are service opportunities all-around us. We need but ask God to lead us to these opportunities and open our eyes to the needs of others. The following story illustrates that, if we desire to find ways to serve others, the Lord will make it possible.

My wife and I moved into a small studio apartment when we were first married. We both had a great desire to serve. One evening after dark, we were trying to decide what we could do to better serve. We kneeled together and asked God to give us the opportunity to help someone. We were humble and eager to serve and our prayer was sincere. We got up from our knees and decided to go outside. As soon as we walked out, we noticed a porch light about three apartments down from us. We remembered that a young couple lived in that apartment but we had no idea who they were. We felt impressed to go knock on their door. A young woman who appeared to be very distraught came to the door and invited us in.

Once we were inside, she began to pour out her heart. Her husband had disclosed that he was interested in an alternative life style. He had packed his belongings and moved out that same day. They had been married about six months. She was devastated and had no family to turn to in her time of trouble. Because we asked the Lord to guide us, we were led to a person who really needed our help at that moment. We provided comfort and help over the next few months so that she could get on her feet. I understood that my problems were minimal in comparison to hers.

It is not likely that we could have planned this act of service on our own. This lonely woman was pouring out her heart to the Lord only three doors away from us. The Lord's spirit was prompting us to answer her prayer in his behalf. Remember to ask the Lord to guide your footsteps in his service. Acts of service take our focus off our pain and heartache and direct our energy toward blessing someone else.

My mission president in Switzerland used to say, "If you live to bless the lives of others, the Lord will give you the power to do so." This power not only blesses others but also heals our soul as we serve.

Most people think that they have some great and world changing purpose in life. There is a reason they think this way. In reality, they really do have a great purpose but it may not be exactly what they think. I always thought I would do some great thing and I was just waiting for God to tell me what it was and I would do it. I just did not realize what "great" meant. Once again God set me on the right path and helped me understand what "great" really meant through a dream.

I dreamed that I came home from work and saw my neighbor taking in the groceries, so I gave her a hand. While walking back across the street, I noticed my next-door neighbor working on his car, so I stopped and helped him. I continued to help other neighbors. As I was returning to the house a very strong impression came to my mind and heart that these were the most important things I could do. These were the "great" things, serving those around me in small ways. Remember the words of King Benjamin in the Book of Mormon, **"when ye are in the service of your fellow beings ye are only in the service of your God" (Mosiah 2:17).** Christ set the example. He went about serving others by helping and loving them. His service was a "great" thing. Our service also can be a "great" thing, and at the same time release his healing power in our lives.

For those who are able to participate and serve in the temple, we can also get extra help in our healing from those deceased persons whom we serve. Elder John A. Widtsoe of the quorum of the twelve apostles said, "These are trying days, in which Satan rages, at home and abroad, hard days, evil and ugly days. We stand helpless as it seems before them. We need help. We need strength. We need guidance. Perhaps if we would do our work in behalf of those of the unseen world who hunger and pray for the work we can do for them, the unseen world would in return give us help in this day of our urgent need. There are more in that other world than there are here. There is more power and strength there than we have here upon this earth. We have but a trifle, and that trifle is taken from the immeasurable power of God. We shall make no mistake in becoming collaborators in the Lord's mighty work for human redemption."[22]

The Church is a wonderful vehicle which allows us to serve our fellowman. Consider for a moment the great opportunity given to each member to serve in the Church. We are all called to fill positions of responsibility and serve our brothers and sisters. Members may be asked to serve for a time in a leadership role and then a few years later be asked to serve in a more supportive responsibility.

While serving in a Bishopric, I remember asking often if I could be released from my present calling to do something else. Eventually, I had a dream that cured me of this request. I found myself on a mountain looking into a great valley and the other counselor in the bishopric was with me. In the valley was a great multitude of people who were serving others. He told me that I was released from my church responsibility and would not be asked to do anything else. I was told I would never have the opportunity to serve again because I was not willing to serve as the Lord had asked me to do. I remember the sinking feeling that came over me as I realized that I would never serve again. Fortunately, I awoke and renewed my determination to do the best that I could where I was assigned.

We also receive the healing influence of the spirit as others serve our needs. Many years ago my wife and I traveled to Prescott, Arizona, to stay at her grandfather's cabin in Groom Creek. We traveled fifteen miles into Prescott to attend our Sunday meetings at the local chapel. When we got into the van after church, we could not start our car because of a broken alternator bracket. I was standing somewhat dejected with the car hood up, and a man approached us to see how he could help.

Once he realized it was something we could not fix, he offered to loan us his new car to drive until we repaired our van. He had purchased the car one week before.

It took about four days for the dealer to get in the part and repair the van. We drove his car the entire time we were at the cabin. I do not know what we would have done if he had not offered his car. We could not afford to rent a car and also have our van fixed. It was interesting to me that he did not know us, other than seeing us at church, and he handed us the keys to his new car without a concern.

As we drove home from our trip, I remember the flood of gratitude that I experienced and the love that I felt for this man and his wife who had first loved us through their service. **"We love him, because he first loved us" (1 John 4:19).** This experience provided healing to my soul because it helped to change my heart and feel love and gratitude toward a complete stranger.

# THE WORD OF GOD

As previously mentioned, people who have suffered abuse or harsh trials often find it difficult to have faith in God. They believe that he will not come to their aid in the present because he did not intervene to protect them in past circumstances. Our lack of faith in Christ is something that may take courage and honest introspection to recognize. Faith in Christ is required to return to the Father. It is so basic to God's plan that it is the first principle of the gospel. Aware of our needs, God provided his words to help unlock our faith in Christ and strengthen our confidence in him. God's words include anything written or spoken by the power of the Holy Ghost.

Elder D. Todd Christofferson, of the twelve apostles, comments on how we can gain faith in God. He said, "Faith will not come from the study of ancient text as a purely academic pursuit. It will not come from archaeological digs and discoveries. It will not come from scientific experiments. It will not even come from witnessing miracles. These things may serve to confirm faith, or at times to challenge it, but they do not create faith. Faith comes by the witness of the Holy Spirit to our souls, spirit to spirit, as we read or hear the word of God. And faith matures as we continue to feast upon the word." [23] Faith is obtained and grows as we feast upon the word of God through study and hearing the inspired words of Christ. The spirit confirms these truths to our soul.

M. Russell Ballard, another modern day apostle, provides a second witness of the power of God's words and their impact on our faith in Christ. He said, "One of the ways I have gained my sure knowledge that Jesus is the Christ is through my study of the scriptures." [24] I am impressed with his wording, "my sure knowledge that Jesus is the Christ." If the word of God brings us to a sure knowledge of Christ, it must certainly bring us to a faith in him prior to our sure knowledge.

The apostle Paul provided yet a third apostolic witness when he said, **"faith cometh by hearing, and hearing by the word of God" (Romans 10:17).** Paul also understood that the power to help us establish faith in God is found in God's word.

So important for the salvation of humanity is the word of God that each of the prophets were commanded to keep a record of the revelations they receive from God. They also kept the writings of past prophets so that their children, their contemporaries, and future generations could be blessed. **"And we had obtained the records which the Lord had commanded us, and searched them and found that they were desirable; yea, even of**

140

**great worth unto us, insomuch that we could preserve the commandments of the Lord unto our children (1 Nephi 5:21).** The ancient American prophet Lehi wrote these words after he left Jerusalem and came to the Americas around 600 BC. He took with him the writings of Moses so that his posterity might preserve the knowledge of the commandments of God.

When the prophet Abraham left the land of Ur he also took with him sacred records. **"But the records of my fathers, even the patriarchs, concerning the right of Priesthood, the Lord my God preserved in mine own hands; therefore a knowledge of the beginnings of creation, and also of the planets, and of the stars, as they were made known to the fathers, have I kept even unto this day, and I shall endeavor to write some of these things upon this record, for the benefit of my posterity that shall come after me" (Abraham 1:31).** He brought with him the writings of his fathers and knew it was important to write the revelations that he received for the blessing of his children.

Historically, people have dwindled in unbelief without the written word of God. We see this with the Mulekites, a group of people who also left Jerusalem and came to America approximately the same time as Lehi and his family. The scriptures tell us, **"and their language had become corrupted; and they had brought no records with them; and they denied the being of their creator; (Omni 1:17**). Without the written word these people were unable to continue a belief in God or safeguard their language from corruption.

Not only is it necessary that we have access to the word but it is vital that we feast upon it. Nephi, the son of Lehi wrote, **"...press forward, feasting upon the word of Christ, and endure to the end, behold, thus saith the Father: Ye shall have eternal life." (2 Nephi 31:19-20)** If faith in Christ is obtained by feasting on the word, it is important to understand what this means. Feasting is generally related to eating. When we come into a dining room to feast on a delicious meal our senses are heightened with smell and sight. As we look over the meal, we can almost taste it before we put it into our mouth. As we eat, we taste and savor each morsel enjoying the flavors and smells. We take it into our bodies to be used for strength and health. We are nourished and satisfied, and we leave the table completely filled. It is a highly enjoyable experience.

To feast on the words of God, we must use our spiritual senses. We must open our hearts and mind to receive the spirit and power of the sacred and holy nature of Christ's words, sensing and recognizing that if we were in God's presence these would be the very words he would speak. We handle and look over them by asking in prayer to feel and understand the spirit of the words, and by reading selected verses and various words and pondering upon their meaning. We savor them by thinking about them in relation to other knowledge we have obtained and by seeking the intended meaning. We digest or internalize the word by meditating on it often and seeking application in our own lives and in the lives of others. We ask God questions and the spirit provides discovery and knowledge. As the spirit witnesses to our soul, our faith increases and we find joy and testimony that adds strength and understanding. Finally in the words of the Savior himself, **"Blessed are they which do hunger and thirst after righteousness: for they shall be filled" (Matthew 5:6).** We ultimately come away from our feasting spiritually filled and completely satisfied.

Feasting on the scriptures provides special blessings that will change our lives and heal our wounded hearts. **"And it supposeth me that they have come up hither to hear the pleasing word of God, yea, the word which healeth the wounded soul." (Jacob 2:8)** Through study and hearing God's word we can find healing for the soul, the type of healing that will bring peace and forgiveness into our lives. I will briefly touch upon some of the ways the word of God specifically blesses those who have been wounded and offended in their heart.

We are promised that if we will feast on God's word we will be filled with the spirit. As we read and ponder the words of Christ, they begin as a very small glow and swell within our breast until we are filled with joy and the spirit of the Lord. The ancient prophet Lehi saw God the Father, his Son, and the twelve apostles of the Lamb in vision. He tells us that the first apostle stood before him, **"...and gave unto him a book, and bade him that he should read. And it came to pass that as he read, he was filled with the Spirit of the Lord" (1 Nephi 1:12).** As Lehi read, he was filled with the converting and changing power of the spirit. It is the spirit of God that fills us and changes our heart and soul to be like that of Christ. The spirit fills us with love for all of God's children and helps us to forgive those that may have offended us. The spirit accompanies the words of Christ and moves us to action and allows us to break free from our own base desires and seek higher ground.

The word of God also heals us by infusing light into a soul that may be struggling in darkness and despair. **"Behold, he changed their hearts; yea, he awakened them out of a deep sleep, and they awoke unto God. Behold, they were in the midst of darkness; nevertheless, their souls were illuminated by the light of the everlasting word;" (Alma 5:7).** The prophet Alma taught that the saints were illuminated by the word of God and filled with his light, uplifted in mind and body, and awakened. To be illuminated means to make clear or to clarify. In chapter 2 we spoke of the importance of the discovery of truth as it relates to emotional healing. When we are illuminated we are awakened to the truth about ourselves, our fellowman, and God. We begin to see from God's perspective and tear down the false beliefs that have haunted our troubled souls. We can focus on our weaknesses that need our attention and apply ourselves to overcoming them with the help of God. The word of God provides clarity through truth.

Illumination carries with it a wonderful feeling of joy, something many of us may not have experienced since early childhood or not at all. **"Thy words were found, and I did eat them; and thy word was unto me the joy and rejoicing of mine heart" (Jeremiah 15:16).** The light that fills our souls infuses into our hearts joy and rejoicing.

Another healing blessing derived from the study of the word of God is that we will be brought before the altar

144

of God. **"By the power of their words many were brought before the altar of God, to call on his name and confess their sins before him" (Alma 17:4).** The word of God can be conveyed and attended with such power and spirit that we are moved to repent and give up our weaknesses and negative attitudes at the altar of God. We cry out as did the people of King Benjamin saying, **"O have mercy, and apply the atoning blood of Christ that we may receive forgiveness of our sins, and our hearts may be purified; for we believe in Jesus Christ, the son of God" (Mosiah 4:2).** It is before this sacred imaginary altar that we give our complete will over to the Savior and allow our will to be swallowed up in his will. We take his name upon us without shame or fear. We experience a rebirth that heals the heart and soul. We turn over our anger and unwillingness to forgive. We give up our pride and selfish need for retribution. We surrender the false beliefs that keep us in destructive patterns of behavior. The word of God effectuates the Atonement and brings it to bear on our lives with power and love.

The giving of our will to God results in the removal of pride. The word of God pulls down our pride. Pride always resides in our hearts when we are unwilling to forgive and let go of past hurt and pain. **"And that he might pull down, by the word of God, all the pride and craftiness and all the contentions which were among his people" (Alma 4:19).** When we feast on the word of God the spirit softens our heart and the truth exposes our weaknesses and helps us see ourselves in relation to God's majesty and strength.

The study of God's word also provides sanctification. **"Sanctify them through thy truth: thy word is truth" (John 17:17).** The study of the scriptures helps us to become a holy and saintly person. It gives us the strength to relinquish addictions and poor habits. We become more and more like our teachers and mentors, Christ and the prophets, because we are focused on their teachings and examples. Our minds gravitate to the things we study and ponder, and we live accordingly. As we become holy, we can stand in the presence of God and man confident and free from the pain of spiritual and emotional torment.

God's word sanctifies our soul as does Christ himself. In writing to the Hebrews Paul says, **"Wherefore, Jesus also, that he might sanctify the people with his own blood, suffered without the gate" (Hebrews 13:12).** Paul tells us that it is through Christ that we are sanctified. The "word of God" sometimes has dual meaning. Christ is also referred to as the "Word of God" in the scriptures. **"And he was clothed with a vesture dipped in blood: and his name is called The Word of God" (Revelations 19:13).** The words of Christ and Christ himself have the same purpose and objective, to bring us back into the presence of God our Father. The scriptures lead us directly to Christ and Christ provides, through the Atonement, the way back to the Father.

The word of God teaches us how to come to the Savior so that we may be transformed into a new creature. Christ holds the power to heal our souls and his words convey that healing balm, inviting and bringing us to him so that we can be washed in his blood and made pure.

The word of God is spiritually powerful because it originates from Christ, from his pure and holy mind and heart. The ancient prophet Nephi confirmed the origin of the scriptures and the writings of the holy prophets when he said, **"And if ye shall believe in Christ ye will believe in these words, for they are the words of Christ" (2 Nephi 33:10).** Christ's words carry power, healing, truth, and light deep into the darkened souls of the children of men. They restore the light of Christ that has dimmed through abuse or sin. They ignite within us remembrances and feelings that we have long forgotten and have been chased far from our hearts. The word connects with our heart and mind because we are forever searching to fill the void that was created when we left the presence of God to come to earth. As we feast upon the words of God, Christ will spark the divinity within our hearts and minds, dress and heal our wounded souls, and bring us to the Father.

# FACING EMOTIONS

We discussed the character of negative emotions in earlier chapters and the importance of dissipating or clearing these emotions. Emotions are physiological realities that occur based on our perceptions. Emotions are a natural part of our make up. In and of themselves they are not good or bad. They are labeled as positive or negative in the sense that the vibratory rate of the emotion's energy may be so low that it does not promote or allow healing. It actually promotes sickness. The higher the vibratory rate of an emotion, the more positive the effect will be on the body and spirit. Thus, some emotions have a negative effect when we choose to hang on to them. If we let go of them quickly, we avoid undesirable effects. The emotions that vibrate at lower rates are emotions like shame, anger, guilt, fear, apathy, grief, and pride.

There are many ways to work on releasing our emotions. One option to clear emotions is through the verbal expression of feelings to the offending party. If we do not reconcile with others, we cannot go to the Lord with full purpose of heart. **"Therefore, if ye shall come unto me, or shall desire to come unto me, and rememberest that thy brother hath aught against thee— Go thy way unto thy brother, and first be reconciled to thy brother, and then come unto me with full purpose of heart, and I will receive you" (3 Nephi 12:23-24).** The Lord expects us to forgive others before we can anticipate his blessings.

When reconciling with another it would be ideal if we could express feelings in a healthy setting when this person is willing to listen and validate our feelings. This is rarely possible since the other party is not willing to participate or is no longer accessible. Most often this process will need to occur during visualization. If it is possible you are very fortunate indeed.

As parents it would be well if we could implement the following steps with our children and spouse so that it becomes a positive way to deal with and move through negative emotions and feelings.

1) Identify the feeling or emotion (See the list of feelings at the end of this chapter). Pay attention to the location in our body where we feel the emotion.

2) Allow ourselves to feel the emotion – experience it. The emotion is hard to clear without feeling it. It is okay to feel emotions. We are intended to feel them.

3) Express the emotion (Properly express it as illustrated below).

I feel _____

when you _____

because I _____

And I need/want _____

For example we might say, "I feel unimportant when you ignore my comments because I have worth and I have a right to be respected by others and I need you to be considerate when I speak to you." It is much more effective than the normal screaming and ranting that takes place in many households. It allows us to avoid attacking and blaming the other person.

4) A final step is to receive validation about our emotion when possible.

If we are on the receiving end of someone expressing their emotions, it is important to validate his or her feelings. This may be difficult because the things they say may be difficult to hear and may make us want to fight back and defend ourselves. If we offer a defense it will not assist the person in releasing the emotion. It will only turn into an argument. Let me give an example:

One of my children came to me and said, "Dad, I never feel like you listen to me when I talk. I feel like you don't really care about my feelings." I immediately went on the defensive by saying that it was not true. I watched his countenance fall. I realized that whether I recognized it or not, it was what he felt, and it was his true experience. I needed to respect and validate his feelings. I stopped myself and said, "I am sorry that I made you feel that way, I will try to be a better listener. Please forgive me." This may have been the first time in his life that he felt like I cared about him. Yes, I had coached his teams, we had been on outings, and I had told him over and over I loved him. When this occurred the barriers fell, and we could communicate much better. This does not mean that this experience undid all of the prior issues between us but it allowed some positive direction in our relationship.

Most families do not allow their children to express their emotions. When they get hurt we say, "Oh buck up." When they feel bad we say, "You'll get over it." When they are mad we just tell them to get over it or we'll give them something to be mad about. It is important to show empathy and understanding and discover what is really going on in their lives. They will trust you with other more important conversations as time goes on if you are concerned about their feelings now. It may make the difference in some very important choices they make in the future.

As mentioned, we do not always have the opportunity to express our feelings to an offending party. The person may be deceased or not willing or able to be with us. What can we do? It is not necessary that this be done in person. In the majority of cases we will not be able to do this in person. The concept of doing things by proxy, representing someone and doing something in their behalf, may help us better understand what I will explain. We have discussed creation and visualization. Here we put it into practice through our mental energy.

We can use similar steps as I just outlined to express our emotions or the spirit may direct us to express our feelings differently. We imagine the offending individual as if he or she was in our presence. This may be difficult because of the strong feelings we may have toward them. We need to imagine them in an altered state, as if they can now see, feel, and understand our point of view. It may be necessary to visualize the Savior beside the person, teaching and helping them to understand.

As we visualize, we identify the feelings we are agonizing over, we allow ourselves to feel the emotion and verbally express our feelings to the person in our imagination. It may help to express our feelings aloud as we go through this process. This may not be enough, and we may need to express our feelings through actions, like the woman I referred to in Chapter 10 who mentally beat up her unfaithful husband. We should focus on one emotion at a time.

In our minds eye, we should pay attention to the reaction of the offending party as we express our feelings and what he may say or feel. We should allow him to apologize and seek our forgiveness and the forgiveness of the Savior. We should let him express his emotions. We should allow him to be comforted physically and emotionally by the Savior. We must allow the light of the Savior to fill our hearts and the heart of the offending person. We should see, feel, and experience all of the things in our mind as if it were actually occurring. As we do this we will probably notice that our visualization will move along without too much effort on our part, and we will spend our time observing and feeling instead of forcing things to happen. In reality, as we go through this process, we are creating spiritually. We are allowing, and in a way, calling upon the Savior's power and love to heal another as well as ourselves. We are implementing the Atonement.

If we are not sure about our feelings and want to find out if we have strong emotions about something, there are a couple of things we can do. If we feel comfortable doing so we can find a trusted friend and tell her our experience aloud. As we recount our experience, we will feel a rise in emotion as we speak of certain aspects of the event. Those are the emotional points of impact, and we can be sure the negative emotions are still affecting our lives. Another powerful method would be to write a letter to God expressing our emotions and telling our story. We just need to start writing and should write whatever comes to our mind and heart. We should read it aloud. As we write it out and read it aloud, we will experience points of emotional impact. We should go back and read it again later and see if any of our emotions have reduced or cleared. Once the emotions subside, throw it away.

Here is another way to help clear emotions that may be incorporated with other methods or completed alone. As we tell or read our experience, we must pay attention to the location in our body where the specific emotions are stored. We will feel these emotions if they are present. In our mind's eye, imagine bringing the emotion out in front of us and seeing it as a shape with a color. By projecting it out in front of us we can allow the light of Christ to come from Christ and surround and penetrate the shape. This exercise wil cause the shape to dissipate and the strength of the emotion reduce.

Sometimes it takes a few minutes to disappear. If it is hard to see the shape disappear, imagine the shape getting so large that the light can easily flow through and around it. This will allow the shape to be more easily absorbed by the light of Christ.

We can visualize anything we desire. That is the beauty of the process. Some people visualize themselves in a very peaceful place where they can meet with the Savior and personally bring out their emotions and problems and hand them to Christ. They see him take these emotions, and they feel the lightness that comes over them as he does so. There is no limit to your imagination.

## List of Negative Emotions

This list is here to give you some ideas as you try to come to terms with what you are feeling.

**Freedom/Control**
Controlled, Imprisoned, Inhibited, Forced, Manipulated, Obligated, Overruled, Powerless, Pressured, Restricted, Suffocated, Trapped

**Love/Connection/Importance**
Abandoned, Alone, Brushed off, Confused, Disapproved of, Discouraged, Ignored, Insignificant, Invisible, Left out, Lonely, Misunderstood, Neglected, Rejected, Unheard, Unimportant, Uninformed, Unloved, Unsupported, Unwanted

## Dignity/Respect/Self-Worth

Ashamed, Beaten down, Criticized, Dehumanized, Disrespected, Embarrassed, Humiliated, Inferior, Insulted, Labeled, Lectured to, Mocked, Offended, Resentful, Ridiculed, Stereotyped, Teased, Underestimated

## Justice/Truth

Accused, Cheated, Falsely accused, Guilt-tripped, Interrogated, Judged, Lied about, Lied to, Misled, Punished, Robbed

## Safety

Abused, Afraid, Attacked, Frightened, Intimidated, Over-protected, Scared, Terrified, Threatened, Under-protected, Unsafe, Violated

## Trust

Cynical, Guarded, Skeptical, Suspicious, Untrusting

# UNITY

In the subconscious mind there is no such thing as the past. It is as if everything that took place in our past is really something that has recently occurred. Dr. Bruce Lipton states that, "the subconscious mind is always operating in the present."[25] When an abusive event occurs in our childhood it imprints and programs our subconscious. It is as if the event just occurred.

To survive our negative emotions we dissociate in some way to cover the pain and still go on with life, especially if the event is traumatic. We grow into adulthood and continue to deal with certain circumstances from the emotional level of a child. The part of us that holds the pain never grows up. This also occurs when people get into drugs. They usually stay at the emotional maturity level they were at when they started using.

People who have been through very abusive events dissociate to such a degree that some of them develop what is referred to as multiple personalities.

156

When the abuse occurred, they may have separated into two or several different parts. For some people, their consciousness is forced to separate from the present situation to deal with the trauma. This is a common experience during ritual abuse, incest, and other extremely abusive circumstances. I have visited with a few individuals who have been able to describe their separation in detail. Because of the split or separation that occurs, many of these individuals have completely blocked the memory of the abuse and have no conscious knowledge of the events. They may still be involved and not even know it. They may have fears or triggers that seem to have no foundation or good explanation. They may lose specific time periods and not remember what they did.

These dissociated personalities or parts are fearful and protective and need to be recovered, healed, and united. There must be unification of all subconscious dissociated parts for a person to gain full healing.

There seems to be some form of separation to a lesser degree with all traumas. This is a condition in which the negative emotions are locked within us at the age of the occurrence. These younger parts of us that are frozen in time need to heal, mature, and become unified with our ideal self. Professional help may be necessary if we suspect we have serious personality separation issues. Be prayerful in selecting a counselor. We also need to ask for the Savior's power of reconciliation or At-one-ment.

There is another unification that is required for us to become whole. This is the synchronization of mind and heart. The heart always wins out, no matter how much mental willpower we exert. You may wonder why Laman and Lemuel, in the Book of Mormon, did not believe in the same way Nephi did? Why, even after seeing miracles, they still murmured? An angel appeared to them and as soon as the angel was gone they began to complain. **"And after the angel had departed, Laman and Lemuel again began to murmur (1 Nephi 3:31).** We ask ourselves, how is this possible?

We later learn that there was a problem with what Laman and Lemuel saw with their eyes and what they believed in their heart. **"And they said: Behold, we cannot understand the words which our father hath spoken concerning the natural branches of the olive tree, and also concerning the Gentiles. And I said unto them: Have ye inquired of the Lord? And they said unto me: We have not; for the Lord maketh no such thing known unto us. Behold, I said unto them: How is it that ye do not keep the commandments of the Lord? How is it that ye will perish, because of the hardness of your hearts?" (1 Nephi 15:7-10).** Their hearts were hard to the truth. They had their own belief system in their heart and it was different from what their eyes had seen.

We operate each day based on the beliefs in our heart. As we mature, we accept new beliefs and mentally tell ourselves that we will follow these new beliefs. The problem manifests when we try to act on these new beliefs, and we find ourselves doing what we have always done. We become frustrated and usually give up trying. We do this because the heart continues to believe based on our original experiences.

No matter what the mind says, no matter how hard we try to exert our will power we will continue to fall back into our same negative patterns and false beliefs. I refer to this quote once again." **For with the heart man believeth unto righteousness" (Romans10:10).** Our hearts control our actions because our true beliefs exist in the heart.

If we become aware of changes we need to make in our lives we will need to change the beliefs in our hearts. Nephi tells us how he did this. "**I did cry unto the Lord; and behold he did visit me, and did soften my heart that I did believe all the words which had been spoken by my father (1 Nephi 2:16).** God is the one that changes our heart.

The scriptures tell us that many do not believe because they have a hard heart. A hard heart cannot be penetrated by the spirit of the Lord and made soft unless we ask God to help us. If our hearts are hard and we are not open to God's love and power, we will not be able to change our hearts to align with our minds once we realize a change is necessary.

Nephi's heart was softened so that he believed with his heart and was able to perform the commandments with faith and diligence, not just knowing what he should do but completely believing in what he should do. **"And it came to pass that I, Nephi, said unto my father: I will go and do the things which the Lord hath commanded, for I know that the Lord giveth no commandments unto the children of men, save he shall prepare a way for them that they may accomplish the thing which he commandeth them" (1 Nephi 3:7).** Nephi's heart had truly been changed.

# CONCLUSION

I have presented many concepts and thoughts related to emotional healing. Progress takes effort and commitment. I invite each person to study and put the word of the Lord to the test. I have tried to support these concepts with scripture so that you might pursue your spiritual healing with confidence in the Savior's promises.

It is true that our experiences may determine our behavior, but once we become aware of why we do what we do, and recognize our irrational behavior and the effect it has upon others and ourselves, we can no longer blame our abusive experiences or the offenses of another for our behavior. We have all been programmed to behave and act in certain ways, but we have the power to change. God can help us do that if we ask specifically for his help. We have the responsibility to stop using our past misfortunes as an excuse and seek healing.

God did not put us here to fail, but to grow and confront the trials of life so that we can become like him. Yes it is hard, but we are more than capable of accomplishing hard things. **"For the power is in them, wherein they are agents unto themselves" (D&C 58:28).** We have the ability to conquer all of life's challenges.

In summary, I have suggested several things we can do to heal. First, we must go before God realizing that we are all sinners. This is not just for those that have committed offense but those that have received offense. We must beg for the grace and power of the Lord Jesus Christ to remove our bitterness and change our hearts. Second, we need to express gratitude for the difficult experiences in our lives and seek learning from them. Third, we must serve others and take the focus off of ourselves, our self-pity and our victim mentality. We must turn our focus outward. Fourth, we must ask for help and answers through prayer, always remembering to be still and listen for God's voice. Fifth, we should feast upon the words of Christ that will bring us to the feet of the Savior for healing and peace. Finally, we must imagine the ideal, always visualizing and imagining what we can become as if we already are that person.

I invoke the blessings of God upon anyone that applies truth with a humble, sincere, and willing heart. May God hear your cries and heal your heart and soul through the healing power of the Atonement of our Savior, Jesus Christ. May God bless you in your journey back to Him. The power of the Atonement can change your life. I invite you to come unto Christ and be perfected in him through his merciful Atonement. I testify before all mankind that Christ lives, he loves us, his promises are true, and he is the Savior and Redeemer of the world.

# APPENDICES

## Ideas and Helps to Overcome
## Negative Behavior

# A.    Healing Concepts

*Many of the ideas mentioned below are things we have discussed in this book. An explanation of some of the items listed below will follow this outline.*

## Recognition

a.    I harbor some unresolved negative emotions and need the healing power of Jesus Christ.

b.    My unresolved negative emotions result in sin, addiction, irrational thoughts or negative patterns of behavior.

c.    Events, stress and/or relationships trigger my negative emotions.

d.    My negative emotions affect self and others.

e.    My emotional pain causes me to operate from a position of weakness and need instead of strength and love.

f.    I am responsible for my own emotional well-being.

g.    I realize that I am the creator of my own environment.

h.    I can only change myself and not others.

## Willingness

a.    I will do what is necessary to heal.

b.    I will be humble and submissive and cast off pride.

c.    I will discuss feelings and emotions in a healthy way and in a safe environment.

d.    I will let down my facade and stop running and hiding.

e.    I will suspend and release judgment of self and others.

f.      I will seek out ways to see things from a different perspective.

## Belief (Hope)

a.      God can and will take away the strong influence of my negative feelings and emotions.

b.      The Savior can heal my addictions and pain.

c.      It is through the Savior's love and Atonement that I am restored to wholeness.

d.      I can love myself and others.

e.      My life can be enjoyable, fulfilling and exciting.

f.      My depression can be overcome.

g.      I can feel compassion for and forgive those who have hurt me.

h.      I can facilitate healing through the Savior according to the righteous imaginations of my heart.

## Knowledge

a.      I understand the relationship of sin and abuse to symptoms and feelings.

b.      I understand the true nature of God's children.

c.      I see the relationship of emotional health to physical health.

d.      I understand the concept of mental exertion and words (faith). As a man thinketh in his heart, so is he.

e.      I understand the relationship of the mind and heart.

f.      I understand principles such as truth, forgiveness, judgment, grace, guilt, suffering, service, unity

g.      I understand Christ's role in healing.

## Identification

a. Utilize the Savior and His spirit.

b. Work on one issue at a time.

c. Identify false beliefs, negative patterns and irrational thoughts.

d. Identify, if possible, the related trauma/abuse.

e. If unable to identify the trauma, identify feelings, location of feelings in the body, colors and shapes of feelings.

f. Identify emotions related to these beliefs and traumas.

g. Identify effects of our actions on ourselves and others.

h. Identify the correct beliefs, patterns and thoughts.

## Faith (Mental Exertion)

a. Quiet the mind (Meditation, Alpha State)

b. Self- Awareness (Focus Attention, Live in the present)

c. Creation (Visualization, Affirmation)

d. Develop image of ideal self.

e. Feast on the Word of God.

## Forgiveness/Replacement

a. Seek new perceptions. (Create love and Compassion)

b. Change the way I see self, others, events, God.

c. Fill the void with the light of Christ and compassion.

d. Predetermine positive behaviors and actions.

e. Replace negative behaviors with positive.

## Maintenance

a. Physical exercise, nutrition, and grooming.

b. Healing log - journal (feelings, successes, recognitions), photos, dream log, goals.

c. Affirmations, negative patterns and false beliefs worksheet.

d. Gratitude for all experiences, service, quiet the mind, suspend judgment.

e. Feast on the Word of God

f. Prayer with visualization.

# B.    Healing Journal

*Many years ago I put together a type of journal or log that has helped contribute to my healing. In the scriptures, the Lord uses the term "remember" many times. This log allows you to do that. These are the things that it might contain:*

**Journal** – Write down thoughts and feelings from the day. This will help you see your progress and may provide a valuable resource for others in the future. You can also see the blessings that the Lord pours out upon you. This allows you to build upon your experiences. As you read about your positive experiences you will recreate positive feelings and emotions.

**Dream Log** – Write down any dreams from the night. Have three columns labeled, 1- What I dreamed, 2- What I think it means, (ask the Lord and put your best guess) 3- The realization of the dream or it's meaning. The third column may or may not materialize but many times it does.

**Positive Photos** – These photos may be of yourself as a baby, a little child, a teenager, a young man or woman, photos of events that bring up good feelings and memories, or photos of others that you have good feelings toward. In other words, collect images that create positive emotions and feelings about yourself and others.

**Affirmations** –These are "I am" statements. For example, an affirmation may be "I am loved by God" or "I am friendly and kind to everyone."

**Negative Patterns & False Beliefs Worksheet** – Identify negative patterns of behavior, identifying the positive alternative, and visualize yourself performing the positive pattern (use all senses). Affirm the positive pattern. Identify false beliefs, identify the true belief or alternative, and visualize yourself believing the truth (use all of your senses). Affirm the true belief. Gain an alternate perception and record it.

**Goals** – Collect pictures that represent your goals, write affirmations, visualize and believe.

# C.    Patterns - Negative vs Positive

*Listed below are a few of the negative patterns and false beliefs that we may develop due to abuse, irrational thoughts, or incorrect teachings of parents and adults. These negative patterns of behavior and false beliefs do not just go away because we have released negative emotions and now feel compassion. We have been doing and thinking these negative things for a long time.*

*Once the bitterness and hurt begins to move on and the heart is changing, we must work to identify negative patterns of behavior and false beliefs. We can now deal with negative patterns from an increased position of strength and an attitude of compassion. Once they are identified, we need to discover what the positive pattern or true belief is in order to replace the old with the new. If we do not implement this with all of our effort and with help from the Savior, we will continue to recreate some of the same negative emotions within ourselves by bringing similar situations into our lives. Just remember to focus on one thing at a time until you feel comfortable and feel like it is something you are gaining control over.*

- **Negative -** I place the blame for my mistakes on others. I use others mistakes and faults as an excuse for my behavior.
- **Positive –** I take full responsibility for my decisions and actions. I alone determine my actions and thoughts.

- **Negative -** I try to control others through guilt, blame, force, fear, and neglect so that they will be or do what I want.

- **Positive** – I allow everyone agency and freedom to chose without ridicule or judgment. I set boundaries when I act responsible and I never criticize or blame. Agency is a gift of God and others do not have a responsibility to meet my needs or make me happy.

- **Negative** - I belittle myself when I make mistakes. I do not allow myself to make mistakes. I must be perfect.
- **Positive** – I base my value on the fact that I am a child of God not on what I have accomplished. Mistakes are a natural part of learning and progression. God loves us in spite of our mistakes.

- **Negative** - I sabotage relationships so that others will not get close enough to hurt me. I gain weight to make myself look unattractive and unwanted. I don't expect relationships to work out.
- **Positive** – I build relationships based on mutual trust, respect, and communication. Future relationships are based on the present, not on past hurtful relationships. I seek out and discover the reasons behind my relationship issues. I can have a healthy relationship with a wonderful person. I deserve to be with someone that loves and cares about me.

- **Negative** - I cover up and protect misdeeds, problems or addictions of loved ones. I need to rescue, or take care of, others with problems.
- **Positive** – I realize that keeping family secrets has negative effects and I allow my family and loved ones to express their feelings openly without ridicule. Problems

are universal and are a part of life and should not be an embarrassment. Others are responsible for the way they think and act.

- **Negative -** I do many things for those outside of my immediate family but neglect my own family.
- **Positive –** My family members are the most important people in my life and deserve the greatest respect and love I can give them.

- **Negative -** I lose interest quickly and cannot stay with a task. I rarely complete a project. I experience repeated failures in many different areas of life. I set unrealistic goals and seldom accomplish them.
- **Positive –** I am capable and successful. I focus and stay interested in the things I need to do. I set reasonable goals and accomplish each one.

- **Negative -** I avoid socialization with family, friends and people in general. I am always running, hiding and drifting with no roots. To avoid embarrassment, I say very little and seldom express opinions.
- **Positive –** I interact positively and courageously in a social setting. I look for opportunities to be with and enjoy others. I make a difference and am a blessing to others.

- **Negative -** I lose control of my emotions easily.
- **Positive –** I control my feelings and emotions by expressing them in a non-accusing, non-threatening, calm manner.

• **Negative -** I am addicted to (Drugs, Alcohol, Smoking, Pornography, Shopping, Sex, Food, Movies, etc.) to cover pain, hurt and loneliness or to feel loved and accepted.

• **Positive –** I turn myself over to the healing power of the Savior and seek in every way possible to heal the pain and free myself from my addictions. My addictions hurt myself and others and I no longer need them to feel good. God can bring joy into my life without the addictions.

• **Negative -** I allow others to take advantage of me and later become angry with myself for allowing it to happen. I compromise my values to gain others acceptance.

• **Positive –** I am of worth and my opinions and feelings are important. I have the maturity and ability to prevent mistreatment from others. I am no longer a child.

• **Negative -** I constantly try to guess what others are thinking of me and I often project negative thoughts on them when the opposite may be true.

• **Positive –** People are generally good and there is no reason for them to think poorly of me or anyone else. There is no way for me to know their thoughts.

# D.    False Beliefs vs Truth

## Love and Self Worth

### False Beliefs

I am not worthy of Love.
Others cannot accept me as I am.
I must change to be loved.
God will not love me if I make mistakes.
I feel love when someone hurts me.
I am a bad person and do not deserve love.
I must be perfect or I am nothing. I must be the best at everything.
Self worth is based on performance.
Self worth is based on others compliments and recognition.
I must be liked and accepted by everyone.
I have nothing to live for.
If I let down my facade, I will not like what I see.
I am a failure and can't do anything right.
Others would be happier if I did not exist.
I stay in an abusive relationship because I deserve it.

### Truth

**John 3:16** For God so loved the world, that he gave his only begotten Son, that whosoever believeth in him should not perish, but have everlasting life.
**Gal 5:14** 14 For all the law is fulfilled in one word, *even* in this; Thou shalt love thy neighbour as thyself.

**1 John 4:8,9,19** He that loveth not knoweth not God; for God is love. In this was manifested the love of God toward us, because that God sent his only begotten Son into the world, that we might live through him. We love him, because he first loved us.

**Romans 13:8** ...for he that loveth another hath fulfilled the law.

**Moses 1:4,6** thou art my son..., My son; thou art in the similitude of mine Only Begotten...

**Moses 1:39** For behold, this is my work and my glory—to bring to pass the immortality and eternal life of man.

**Psalms 82:6** Ye are Gods, and all of you are children of the most High.

**Romans 8:16-17** The Spirit itself beareth witness with our spirit, that we are the children of God: And if children, then heirs; heirs of God, and joint-heirs with Christ ...

**Genesis 1:27** So God created man in his *own* image, in the image of God created he him; male and female created he them.

## Judgment of Self and Others

### False Beliefs

I am the only one that feels this way.

These things have only happened to me, no one else.

My own trauma has had no effect on my emotions or thinking.

Others should be kinder and more compassionate.

Others should pay for their abuses.

Others do not think clearly or rationally.

I will always be affected by past trauma.

Others do not mean it when they say good things about me.

I have hurt so many people, I can never make it right or be forgiven.

I know what others are thinking about me.

## Truth

**D&C 58:42** Behold, he who has repented of his sins, the same is forgiven, and I, the Lord, remember them no more.

**Matthew 1:1-2** Judge not, that ye be not judged. For with what judgment ye judge, ye shall be judged: and with what measure ye mete, it shall be measured to you again.

**Mosiah 29:12** Now it is better that a man should be judged of God than of man, for the judgments of God are always just, but the judgments of man are not always just.

**Romans 14:13** Let us not therefore judge one another any more: but judge this rather, that no man put a stumblingblock or an occasion to fall in his brother's way.

**D&C 64:10** I, the Lord, will forgive whom I will forgive, but of you it is required to forgive all men.

## Responsibility and Relationships

### False Beliefs

I am responsible for others behaviors.

Others should know what I am feeling.

Others should recognize and meet my needs.

I cannot say "no" to others.

Others determine my happiness or sadness.

I must control others through guilt, force or fear.

I cannot control my emotions and feelings.

Others should fix my problems and anger.

My actions and feelings only affect myself.

I must rescue all those that are weak and suffering,

Because of my past I cannot change how I feel or act.

I feel love when I experience pain in a relationship.

I must be better than the opposite sex or I am weak.

Relationships will always end in abandonment and hurt.

## Truth

**John 8:32** ...the Truth shall make you free...

**D&C 93:29-30** Man was in the beginning with God, Intelligence. Or the light of truth... truth is independent in that sphere in which God placed it, to act for itself,...

**D&C 58:28** For the power is in them, wherein they are agents unto themselves.

## Faith in God and Others

## False Beliefs

God did not protect me when I couldn't protect myself; I cannot trust God in the future.

God will cast me off if I am not perfect.

I cannot trust anyone.

God only answers my prayers when he feels like it.

I can only depend on myself.

## Truth

**Joshua 23:10-11** ...for the Lord your God, he it is that fighteth for you, as he hath promised you. Take good heed therefore unto yourselves, that ye love the Lord your God.

**Romans 4:20-22** He staggered not at the promise of God through unbelief; but was strong in faith, giving glory to God; And being fully persuaded that, what he had promised, he was able also to perform. And therefore it was imputed to him for righteousness.

**2 Nephi 10:17** For I will fulfill my promises which I have made unto the children of men.

**D&C 82:10** I, the Lord, am bound when ye do what I say; but when ye do not what I say, ye have no promise.

The following form is a worksheet that can be used to help replace negative emotions and false beliefs and provide an outline for addressing them. We must replace with good all that is negative if we intend to affect others in a positive way. This worksheet also allows you to work on one thing at a time and not deal with everything at once. There is an example included to help you see how it can be applied.

# E.    Patterns And Beliefs Worksheet

**Negative Pattern**

**False Belief**

**Replacement Pattern and Belief**

**Related Trauma**

**Related Feelings**

**Visualization**

**Affirmation**

**Altered Perception or Revealed Learning**

## F.     Worksheet Example

**Negative Pattern**    *I try to control others through guilt, blame, force, fear, neglect, etc… so that they will be or do what I want.*

**False Belief**    *Others should recognize and meet my needs. Others determine my happiness or sadness.*

**Replacement Pattern and Belief**    *I listen to others and have empathy by placing myself in their position. If I were in their shoes, how would I want to be treated and how do I feel when I am controlled? I am responsible for my own needs and happiness.*

[1]**Related Trauma**    *Never allowed to make decisions while growing up. No one listened to my ideas. I never felt important.*

**Related Feelings**    *Frustrated, controlled, powerless, unimportant.*

[2]**Visualization**    *I imagine myself expressing my feelings to parents, older siblings and friends and each one listening attentively by validating my feelings, valuing my opinion and allowing me to make my own choices (visually and verbally). **These individuals may not be like this in real life, but as you visualize you want to see them as their ideal self.** I see my ideal self, listening to others, and validating their feelings and opinions. I see my ideal self, respecting their ideas and feelings. I see the Savior and his attitude toward my thoughts and feelings, and his attitude toward the thoughts and feelings of others. I imagine his light and love going out to each person within my imagination. I imagine Him healing each person in the image. I ask the Savior to teach me what I need to know*

and learn to help me change. What truth can you teach me that will help me forgive and change my heart?

**Affirmation**   *I am important and I am free to express and exercise my freedom of choice. I allow everyone his agency and freedom to chose without ridicule. I respect others' opinions and desires and allow them the freedom to make choices independent of me.*

[3]**Altered Perception or Revealed Learning**   *I could see and feel that each person I visualized had their own issues with self-worth. Many had grown up in very negative or abusive circumstances themselves. Others were focusing on themselves and unable to meet my needs when I was younger. When the Savior approached them I could see the compassion he had for them and their feelings of regret and sorrow for many of the attitudes and thoughts they held. I noticed that the Savior loves and gathers in everyone with his love and healing power. We were all the same in his eyes. He told me that I had this experience so that I could learn to be understanding of others feelings and break the negative patterns so that my children would grow up in greater light and knowledge.*

[1] **You may not be able to identify the trauma so just identify the feelings and where they may be located in the body.**

[2] **Find a quiet place where you can be alone and use any basic method of relaxation. If you are not familiar with any techniques, you can find several different ones on the internet.**

[3] **This is what you learn from your visualization. It may be a different perspective you have gained about yourself, others or a situation. It is generally revealed personal truth. It may come from a feeling, an image, an action, or from the things that the Savior tells you as you ask for his guidance.**

# G.    Bibliography

Scriptural Citations are included in the body of the text. Quotations are selected from all the standard works of The Church of Jesus Christ of Latter Day Saints. The standard works include the following books:

The Holy Bible - King James Version
The Book of Mormon
The Doctrine Covenants
The Pearl of Great Price

**CH 1**    [1] *Teachings of the Prophet Joseph Smith,* sel. Joseph Fielding Smith [Salt Lake City: Deseret Book Co., 1976], p. 121; see also Bruce R. McConkie, Mormon Doctrine [Salt Lake City: Bookcraft, 1966], p. 60.

**CH 2**    [2] Brigham Young, *Journal of Discourses*, Vol 14, p. 160.

**CH 3**    [3] David Viscot, *The Viscot Method*, Houghton Mifflin Co., Boston, 1984, p. 54.
[4] Bruce H. Lipton Ph.D, *The Biology of Belief*, Elite Books, California, 2005, p. 163.

**CH 5**    [5] George G. Richie M.D., *Return From Tomorrow,* Baker Publishing Group, Grand Rapids, MI, 1978 p. 58.
[6] Jeffrey R. Holland, *For Times of Trouble*, New Era, October 1980.

**CH 8**    [7] Journal for the Scientific Study of Religion, Vol. 36, No. 1 (March, 1997), pp. 25-43.
[8] John Taylor, *Deseret News: Semi-Weekly,* August 21,1883, p. 1.

**CH 9**    [9] *Lectures on Faith*, Desert Book Company, Salt Lake City, UT, 1985, p 61, Item 3.
[10] James Allen, *As a Man Thinketh*, 1903, Introduction.
[11] George G. Richie M.D., *Return From Tomorrow,* Baker Publishing Group, Grand Rapids, MI, 1978, p. 53.
[12] Betty J. Eadie, *Embraced by the Light*, Gold Leaf Press, Placerville, CA, 1992, p. 59.
[13] Napoleon Hill, *Think and Grow Rich*, Fawcett Crest Book, 1960, p. 14.
[14] Bruce H. Lipton Ph.D, *The Biology of Belief*, Elite Books, California, 2005, pp. 139-140, also, Moseley, J.B., K. O'Malley, et al. (2002). "A Controlled Trial of Arthroscopic Surgery for Osteoarthritis of the Knee." New England Journal of Medicine 347(2): 81-82.

**CH 10**    [15] Spencer Kimball, *Miracle of Forgiveness*, Bookcraft, Inc., Salt Lake City, UT, 1969, p. 263.

[16] Denver Snuffer, Jr., *The Second Comforter*, Mill Creek Press, LLC, Salt Lake City, UT, 2006, pp. 275-276.

**CH 11** [17] Snow, Biography of Lorenzo Snow, p. 46.

[18] History of the Church of Jesus Christ of Latter Day Saints, Vol 6, p 305.

[19] Lincoln Barnett, *The Universe and Dr. Einstein*, 1948, p 64

[20] *The Teachings of Spencer W. Kimball*, Bookcraft, Inc, 1982, p 32.

**CH 14** [21] Merlin R. Carothers, *Prison to Praise*, Escondido, CA, 1970, pp. 98-99.

**CH 15** [22] Elder John A. Widtsoe," in *Conference Report, April 1943*, 37-39.

**CH 16** [23] Elder D Todd Christofferson, *Ensign, May 2010*, p. 35, "The Blessing of Scripture".

[24] M. Russell Ballard, *Ensign, May 1987*, p. 15, "Keeping Life's Demands in Balance".

**CH 19** [25] Bruce H. Lipton Ph.D, *The Biology of Belief*, Elite Books, California, 2005, p. 169.

If you wish to contact the author,
comments and observations are welcome
at the following email:

drporter21@gmail.com